Man of the House

A Memoir

by

Dr. Colm McAindriu

DORRANCE
PUBLISHING CO
EST. 1920
PITTSBURGH, PENNSYLVANIA 15238

The contents of this work, including, but not limited to, the accuracy of events, people, and places depicted; opinions expressed; permission to use previously published materials included; and any advice given or actions advocated are solely the responsibility of the author, who assumes all liability for said work and indemnifies the publisher against any claims stemming from publication of the work.

All Rights Reserved
Copyright © 2022 by Dr. Colm McAindriu

No part of this book may be reproduced or transmitted, downloaded, distributed, reverse engineered, or stored in or introduced into any information storage and retrieval system, in any form or by any means, including photocopying and recording, whether electronic or mechanical, now known or hereinafter invented without permission in writing from the publisher.

Dorrance Publishing Co
585 Alpha Drive
Pittsburgh, PA 15238
Visit our website at *www.dorrancebookstore.com*

ISBN: 978-88-85272-18-7
eISBN: 978-8-8852-7674-0

To the newborn, the
father babbles language noise, while

the child with its pure intellect scans the universe...

Try to go
inside the infant's vast

wordlessness, which is the same as the silence of a teacher.
Criticism and mistrust have

a small range. Where there is only the face of God, all
judging of betrayal and

disobedience fades.

— Rumi

Inside my home, an All-Pervading Darkness stood heavily, like stagnant water deep inside a steel-covered well, and reeked from the poop and pee of my siblings' dirty Birds-Eye baby diapers. My home was a different kind of room than my kindergarten room, and between the two rooms was the Doorsill where She lived deeper than deep inside an ever-shifting mixing of forms and the deepening sounds of Music. Feeling Her was be-ing. Her memory, then as now, extended and extends, expanded and expands me inside the Whatness of Her. Choices and willpower are not here. Her friendship is. I was, and continues be-coming, Her story. Me is a metaphor. A body is a metaphor, as in a body of beliefs. Inside Her friendship words do not exist, only the Music and the Danc-ing. Those, too, are metaphors. Later I learned to dance to human forms of music. That learning was a kind of be-ing, an invitation to return to the Green Lady, God's wife. Sometimes, She comes out of the River of Life and touches me through a human lady. Other times, She just seems to stay Home in Felt feelings of Mysteries, and God visits me through other forms and smells, and tastes, and colors, depths, expanses and fluid presences. God and Goddess live in the same House, and They seem to do things through humans, animals and rocks, and birds and mountains, and wind and water move to help me to remember Them. They are my only Home beneath the Doorsill, out beyond and below beliefs, groups, violence, complaints, bragging, exhibitionism, arrogance, ignorance, and noise.

    Wherever I go, I move round Him.
    All I *achieve* is His service.
        — Kabir

Chapter 1

This is my story. My dad walks out on us, and I am three. He never looks back. Now I am age four. It is a dusty afternoon in 1948, and Mother is taking me with her to buy food. She has crowned me Man of the House and said she is going to enroll me in kindergarten class at the St. Andrews Church real soon. I feel my shoulders getting strong, and my chest feels big now. She says I am a man. And I've got to protect her and my brother, too. We walk out of our house front door and turn right onto the gravel road. Mother clutches my right hand and pulls me along. We soon turn left onto the concrete sidewalk, and she says, "Keep real quiet! *White people live over there*," pointing to the right, "*and we can't upset the White people.*" She had told me that as Man of the House, I must always walk on the outside when I am with "a lady" to protect her. She says I've got to be a gentleman.

We are going to town now, and I am real happy. Maybe she will buy me something. As soon as we turn left on the sidewalk, I see nice, clean, big white houses on our right side, and Mother says, "White people live in those houses." She raises her finger to her lips and says, "Shhhhhhhheeeeeeeh," like don't say anything. I've got to keep real quiet now. "White people will kill Black folks if they make noise," she says. We walk faster and faster. I can see Highway 61 ahead of us. We turn right now, and Highway 61 and the railroad track are on our left side. Mother squeezes my hand really tight and says, "*Don't look at that White girl coming toward us! Keep your eyes on the ground! Do you hear me?!*"

Man of the House

I say, "Yes, ma'am," and look down after I take one little glance at her. She is pretty, and I want to play with her.

"Let's get off the sidewalk and let *the White people pass by*!" she says, and pushes me off on to the grass to the left. The lady and her daughter come close, and I look at the girl from the corner of my eyes and see her looking back at me, with her head down, too. Mother hisses, "I told you *not to look at that girl! White people will kill you!*" It's too late. Mother walks faster, and I have to run to keep up with her. Soon, we get close to town. There is a big white car parked on the left side of us. There is a man in the car. He looks like a real big man, 'cause he has a big hat on his head, and the hat looks like it is touching the top of the car. Mother tells me to tip-toe so we don't wake up the policeman in the big white car. I look back on the right side, and there are lots of cars in one spot. I ask her why they have so many cars over there. She says they sell cars there. It is Robert's Chevrolet. She tells me that the big building next to it is the courthouse. We cross the highway at the traffic light, and Mother stops. Her grip on my hand is really tight now, and I am hurting.

She says, "You see that spot over there under that light?"

I say, "Yes, ma'am."

She stares down at me, and I feel the heat of her eyes. I keep looking up at her, and she says, "I am only going to tell you this one time, and you had better remember what I say." She points her finger to the traffic light now and tells me again, "You see that spot right over there under that light?!" My hand is hurting, and tears are running down my face. Water is in my eyes, and I can't see much 'cause she is hurting me. She is squeezing my hand so, so tight, and I hurt really bad. "There were some White men.... They had two pick-up trucks backed up to each other. There was a little space between the two trucks...enough space for the men to sit on the backs of their trucks and talk to each other.

"Then they saw a Black man coming from one of the stores, and they called him, 'Come here, boy!' and he went to see what they wanted. When he got over to the men, they made him lay face down on the ground between the two trucks. Then they took ropes and double-tied his feet to the back of one truck, and they double-tied another rope under his arms and tied that rope to the back of the other truck. They were laughing when they got in the trucks, and that Black man was begging for his life. They just kept laughing and drove off in different directions and tore that man's body apart. *Then they drug his body parts all over town till it ripped apart*!

"*Do you hear me?!*"

I say, "Yes, ma'am."

Then, she says, "I told you not to look at that White girl back there and *you did it anyway! White folks kill Black boys when they look at White girls! Do you hear me?!*" I say that I hear her. My hand is hurting really bad. And I remember my dad left home when I was three years old, and I want to ask her if they killed him. But Mother's eyes are red from crying, and she is mad because I looked at the pretty girl. "*White folks might want to castrate you tonight for looking at that girl back there!* White people will *kill Black boys for looking at White girls.*" I am hurting and scared. I do not know what castrate is. I just know it sounds like something that might hurt really, really bad, and I know Mother is angry, and I had better not ask her anything right now.

We go on to the food store on the other side of the railroad tracks. Everything is close together, and there are lots and lots of cans and buckets and sacks of food, and some jars of food too. A White man is standing in the front of the store with a machine on the counter, and he is not even looking at us. I ask Mother, "Who is that man?" and she says, "He owns the store, and he is going to sell us the food we put in this basket. Now push the basket for me, and I'll put some food in it for us to take home." I push the basket, and she is taking things off the shelves and putting them in the basket. She keeps walking and getting things, putting them in the basket, and she is not talking—just looking and picking things and putting them in the basket. Then we go to the big counter, and she takes everything out of the basket, puts them on the counter with the machine. The man is smiling at me, and he says hello to Mother, and she looks down and says, "Hello, sir." He pulls one thing and pushes buttons on the machine, then he gets another one and hits the machine button, and again till he finishes. Now he is putting each thing in a big brown paper bag. Mother gives him some money, and they smile to each other before we leave the store. Mother keeps her head down when she smiles, and the man just looks at her, and he smiles at me. Now we go back home the same way we came to town. I am looking for the pretty girl, and I do not see her.

Man of the House

We get back home, and I am still scared. I crawl underneath the house where it is quiet and dark. I fall asleep and dream of the White girl. I wake up and bump my head on the bottom of the house. I am sweating and scared. I wonder if the White men are coming to castrate me tonight. I am scared, and my heart is beating really fast. Maybe they killed my dad. When I come out from under the house, it is dark outside. I am scared and worried about my dad, and I sneak back inside of the house.

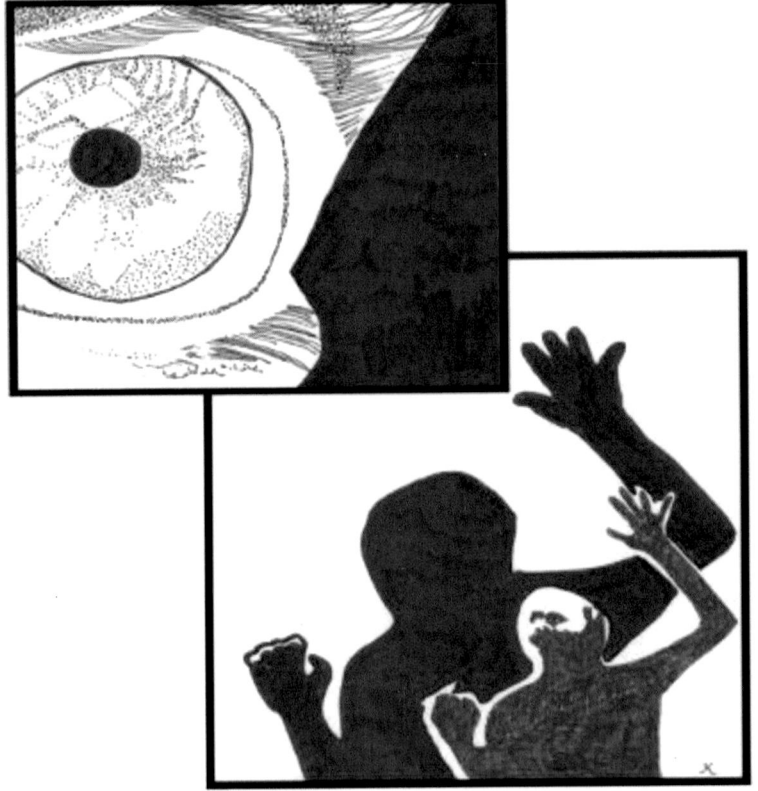

Art by: Kinaesthetics, LLC

Mother sees me come in the house and yells, 'Where have you been?' I tell her and she grabs the extension cord and begins beating me. She tells me to stop running from her and I keep running because she hurts me. Then she smiles and I want her to love me. Mother then starts telling me, "You and I are going to be like *brother and sister*." I feel special when she says that. Mother tells me to put my younger brother to bed early so she and I can drink some Folgers Coffee and talk. While I put my brother to bed, Mother starts the coffee on the stove, and when I finish getting him to bed, she gets the coffee ready and starts pouring it and mixes sugar and coffee cream into it. The coffee is strong. Sometimes she jokes, "It's going to make hair grow on your chest!" We laugh. She tells me stories about the men she likes or has fun with, that my Dad had gone off and married another lady without getting a divorce from her, and that he is a "bigamist"; and she says, "If I ever see a man drowning, *I'll pour some vinegar down his throat!*" She stares through my skin every time she says that.

NOTE: In 2008 I moved back to Shelby and lived there for about 2 years for the purpose of verifying the most challenging stories my mother told me as a child. I interviewed three elderly ladies who knew my mother well and, after telling each of them this lynching story, I asked them if they knew about that event or not? Alarmed, each lady, ages 84, 89, and 94, said "No." and two said, "Absolutely NOT!!" I was stunned that my mother had lied against an entire ethnic group of people; yet I knew that that story may have saved my life. I was 11 years old when 14-year-old Emmett Till was abducted at gun-point and lynched about 15 miles from my home.

Chapter 2
Mother's Prayer

*Love and tenderness are human qualities,
anger and lust are animal qualities. — Rumi*

Mother tells me stories about my great granddad who was a senator. She says that he would not even take his kids to get an ice cream cone. He's White, and his maid, Freda, is Black, so to take his kids out in public would probably end his political career in those days. Mother says that girls are made out of rice, spice, and everything nice, and boys are made out of rats, snails, and puppy-dog tails. Mother says she prayed to God to give her a *girl* for her firstborn, but God knows best; and she says she will make me do everything she was going to make a girl do, 'cause if she had a girl, they could have girl talks. Then she says that she told her friend, "I keep saying *my oldest boy should have been a girl with that good hair he's got!* Then I told him that if you kiss your elbow, you'll turn into a girl! That's what I told him, and I told him that 'you poor thing, you tried to do it, too!' I always wanted my firstborn to be a girl so I'd have somebody to talk to, but the Lord knows best, and He gave me a boy! *I sure wanted you to be a girl*, though!" I started wondering if it would hurt a lot if I cut my penis off. Some nights I lie in bed with my hand covering my penis to see how I would look and wondering how to get my penis cut off so Mother would be happy. I start having nightmares with blood all over me, and I am dying in these dreams.

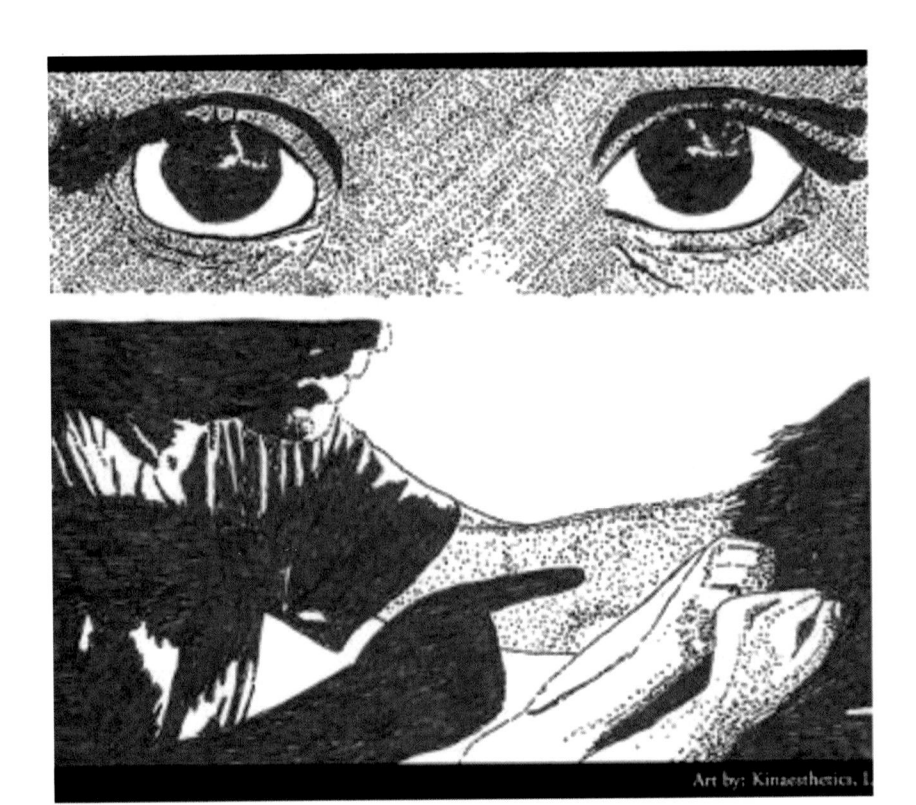

Sometimes she says, "White men don't kill Black girls, just boys!" I'd look at my penis and think about how it could get me killed, and if I had just been born a girl, I would live a long time. The more I think about things like this, the more I want to see how a girl is made so I will know how to make myself okay, live a long time, and make Mother happy. Besides, men, she says, are liars. They always promise to do things for her, but never did. And they cheated on her, too. I do not know what cheating is now. Mother tells me that when her cousin went to Detroit, he promised to send for her so she could go to nursing school and get a good job, and then her brother, Brute promised her that when he got to Kansas City, he would send for her. They lied to her. The Bible says, "Do not tell lies!" "It's getting late. Go to bed," she says. "The stork's gonna bring you a little baby sister or brother soon."

The stork keeps bringing babies to our house. Our house is noisy, dirty, and smells like baby urine and poop. When it rains, our house smells real bad. Mother

Man of the House

yells a lot, the babies cry, and I want to go away to a quiet place to be *alone*. She makes me stay in the house most of the time to learn how to wash dishes, clean the babies, and keep cleaning the whole house all day. Sometimes she tells me stories about Tar Baby and nasty Black men. Then early one morning, she wakes me up, yelling, "Get up and get your clothes on! Your Uncle Brute and Aunt Delight are here to take you to Kansas City! Put all your clothes in a bag and get in here!" I jump out of bed and, wet from peeing while sleeping, put on my blue jeans and shirt over the wet clothes and hope they cannot smell the pee in my clothes. I do not know what is an Uncle or an Aunt. I do not know what is a Kansas City. I am scared Mother does not want me anymore, that maybe she does not love me. I walk into the front room where she is, standing with two other adults, and she tells me, "This is your Uncle Brute and Aunt Delight. They want a son, and you are going to Kansas City with them! Now, go with your Uncle Brute and Aunt Delight!" Crying, I go with the big man and the lady. The Uncle tells me to get in the back seat of the car. It is still dark outside, and I get in the big, black car, looking back at Mother and our house. Daylight is coming, and I am crying. The back seat is cold, and I lie down and fall asleep.

The Uncle wakes me up when we get to the Kansas City and tells me to come with him and the Aunt Delight. We walk on the white-looking ground he calls "concrete" and upstairs to their apartment. He puts a "fold-away bed" on the kitchen floor for me, then we eat food, and they go away to another big room. I get in bed, and when I wake up, the Uncle takes me downstairs to a Ms. Meadows. He tells her that I am the "baby" he wants her to watch. Ms. Meadows is very nice and tells me to go and play under a tree so she can watch me. It is dark when the Uncle comes and takes me back to the kitchen. The Aunt feeds me and tells me to go to bed. I wake up hearing the Aunt screaming, "Oh, God, Brute, please don't hit me no more!" WHOOP, WHOOP! FLOOP! I hear the sounds of the Uncle punching the Aunt and her fall on the floor.

    I run into the room and scream, "Uncle Brute, *please don't hit Aunt Delight!*" He turns to me with cold, red-looking eyes and says, "You little *Bastard*! Whut chu doin' watching?!" He grabs me by the shirt collar, drags me across the floor, and tosses me in the clothes closet on top of a lot of shoes. Clothes hang over my face in the dark closet, and I try to make them get off my face and head. I hear the lock click in place and the sounds of beating and screaming, and cover my ears and cry. I fall asleep. It is quiet when I wake up and hear the Uncle unlocking the door and yelling at me to get up and get ready to go back to Shelby. He takes me back to my mother's house and tells me to get out of his car. I go to the front door and knock as the Uncle drives away. No one answers the door and I go inside. The house is almost dark. I find some left-over bread on the stove, eat some of it, go to bed, and wait for Mother to come home.

I am still scared about my dad. Next morning, Mother wakes me up. "Lord, it's three o'clock already," she says, getting ready to go to work. "He brought you back, huh?" and walking past me, she says, "Check on the babies and see if they need their diapers changed and come in the kitchen with me." I wet the bed, and it is cold getting up because the air hits me when I raise the covers. "Hurry up!" Mother yells at me. Soon she makes me walk out on the front yard with her so she can wait for Mr. Wagner and his wife, Ms. Smalls; they are our neighbors. He takes mother to the cotton field. He comes and she goes away to work, and I go back inside and get in bed. When the sunlight wakes me up, I start cleaning the house. I am still scared my dad might be dead, like Mother said. My brother Will is scared too, and he stays close to me. The baby, Sav, is sleeping. I take Will with me outside to look for four-leaf clovers so we can get lucky, like Mother said, and she will not have to go to work anymore. We sit on the grass in the back yard. Mostly we just have dirt and little patches of grass in the backyard, and the front yard, too. Mother told me long time ago what worms look like before they start to be butterflies, and I know what they look like when they are getting out of the little shell, too. While we look for four-leaf clovers, I tell Will about the worms and butterflies.

Then the baby starts crying and we go back inside. A little mouse looks out at us from a hole in the wall on the other side of the living room. I run in the kitchen and get some breadcrumbs and throw them over to the hole for the mouse. It runs away. Will is laughing at the mouse. It comes back and runs for the bread. We watch the mouse, and it looks back at us like it is scared, too. A screeching sound comes from the kitchen, and I am scared because

Man of the House

Mother said that the Boogeyman and ghosts might come in the house if we are bad and we cannot see them. We can only hear the door move when they come to get us. I look for the ghost out of the corner of my eye. I do not see anything. She said that the Boogeyman might look like a shadow on the wall and get bad boys and eat them. I am the Man of the House, and I am not supposed to be scared. Maybe I just think I am scared, that's all. I go in the kitchen, and the back door is open. The screen door is sagging, and the wire on it is torn and waving in the air. Lots of times flies come in the house through the holes in the screen door. I do not see anything, and the wind blows. I watch the screen door move out and back, screeching. Now I know it is the screen door making the sounds like ghosts and the Boogeyman. My heart is beating real fast, and it is getting dark outside. Mother always comes home when it is real dark, and she has shown me how to light the kerosene lamp. I have to do it just right, because she says it will blow up and kill us if I do not do everything like she says for me to do. I have to do this every evening when Mother goes to the cotton fields. I do not like to be home in the dark when Mother is gone, and I do not like to clean diapers. The diapers smell nasty, and I have to dump the big poop out and wash them in the tub on the washboard. She whips me when I do not clean the babies, feed them, and clean the house, and I have to make sure the babies do not put anything in their mouths, too. I have two baby brothers now. One is drinking milk and he cannot talk yet. It is real dark when Mother comes home. She says she is tired and hungry. I go in the kitchen and get her food to eat and some water. Then she falls to sleep.

Her face, hands, and clothes are dusty and dirty from working in the cotton fields. She wears pants under her dress and a hat on her head when she goes to the cotton field, and they are dirty too when she comes home. After a little while, she wakes up and tells me to check the babies and make sure they are okay and put them to bed. When I get back in the kitchen, she is patting her right leg in rhythmic beats to the same kind of rhythms that we clapped to songs in church one time. "Come on!" she says, "Let's sing!" Her eyes are smiling. She takes off her shoes, pulls the dusty scarf off her hair, and begins patting both legs with her hands in a heart-beating rhythm and singing "Dem Dry Bones."

"Dem dry bones," she sings, patting both legs. "Dem dry bones," and I start singing with her and patting my legs and tapping my feet against the floor.

Man of the House

The floor is my drum and the pats against my legs make a lighter note.

>Dem dry bones! Dem bones!
>Dem, dem, dem, dry bones!
>Dem dry bones!
>Dem dry bones!
>Lordy, Lordy, dem bones!!!

>My foot bone's connected to my leg bone,
>My leg bone's connected to my, my knee bone,
>And, my knee bone's connected to my, my thigh bone,
>My thigh bone's connected to, to, to my back bone!

"That's it, baby!" Mother shouts. "You've got it!" Smiling and picking up the song where she left off and patting her legs:

>My back bone's connected to my neck bone,
>And my neck bone's connected to, to my head bone,
>I feel it in my bone, bones!
>Oooooooh, oh Lordy, Lordy, dem bones!

>Dem bones, dem bones gonna walk aroun'
>Dem bones, dem bones, gonna walk aroun'
>Dem bones, dem bones, gonna walk, walk, walk aroun'
>Oh, Lordy, Lordy, dem bones, dem bones!

"Come on! Let's do it one more time!"

>My head bone's connected to my neck bone,
>And my neck bone's connected to, to, to my back bone!
>My back bone's connected to, to, to my thigh bone!
>My thigh bone's connected to, to, to my knee bone,
>My knee bone's connected to, to, to my leg bone,
>And my leg bone's connected to, to, to my foot bone!

Man of the House

    Oh, Lordy, Lordy, dem bones, dem bones, dem dry bones!

Sweat is running down the sides of her face, and she stops singing. The house is rocking, and my feet keep drumming the floor. I pat my legs and sing on and on till Mother says, "Come with me in the kitchen. We've got to make dinner." I run behind her, singing, "Dem bones, dem dry bones!"

    "What are we going to cook, Mother?" I ask.

    She stops, turns to me, and says softly, "We are going to *prepare* food for dinner; we do not *cook* food. We *prepare* it." She starts singing again,

> I feel it in my bones!
> My head bone's connected to my neck bone
> My neck bone's connected to my back bone!

Looking down at me, she says, "We're going to have neck, neck, neck bones and, and, and turnip greens, greens, greens! My neck bone's connected to…" She laughs and begins washing dishes and looking in the ice box. "You know, I was about your age, in 1929, when the stock market crashed, and Mama had a garden. We had food from the garden," she says. "Come on, let's sing: Dem bones, dem . . . What's that sound I hear?!" It was the sound of dogs barking in the distance. My brothers are sleeping, and Mother blows out the kerosene lamp and tells me to sit at the table with her in the dark. The house is pitch-black dark. "A prisoner might have gotten out of Parchman," she whispers. I hear dogs barking, crickets singing, and frogs croaking. The night is dark everywhere. The sounds of the barking dogs fade, and the crickets and frogs keep singing. "When you hear those dogs barking like that, always put out the light," Mother says, feeling her way through the dark in search of the kerosene lamp and matches. "We do not want the police coming here looking for prisoners with those big bloodhounds and guns. They might think we're hiding a prisoner in here." She finds the lamp and I get the matches and give them to her. One of the babies starts crying.

    "Here are the matches, Mother," I say, giving the small box to her.

    Lighting the lamp, she says, "Go check on the baby to see if he is wet. You might need to change the diaper."

Man of the House

"His diaper is nasty, Mother," I complain.

"*Clean* him!" she says, "And *wash* the diaper. We don't have many diapers, so you've got to wash the dirty one so it can dry before somebody else starts crying." Somebody is burning sticks and grass next door when I go outside to wash the diaper. A bug flies against the torn sagging screen door and falls back on the ground. "Lightning bugs are flying all over the yard, Mother! I got one! Do you wanna see it?"

"Yes!" she says, coming to the door. "Don't squeeze it. There is another one over your head! Now, finish cleaning the diaper and hurry back inside before the Boogeyman gets you! The ghosts come out at night, too!" The hair on the back of my neck gets stiff. I drop the lightning bug, hurry cleaning the diaper, and run back inside the house. The Boogeyman and ghosts are sneaky, and Mother says that no one ever gets a chance to see the ghosts before they get you. Ghosts come from the graveyard after people die, she says.

I finish the baby and go back in the kitchen and sit down in a straw-bottom chair next to Mother. She brings a cup of coffee and sits down, and then she pours a little in another cup for me. "*Drink slow,*" she says, "the coffee is *hot* and might *burn your mouth*. When you grow up and drink coffee, it will put some hair on your chest. Run in and see if the babies are sleeping and hurry back!" I jump up and run through the dark house to the bedroom, check on the babies, and they are snoring. "I'm going to take you to the cotton field tomorrow so you can help me to make some money. Mr. Wagner told me that he's going to a different field tomorrow where they pay three dollars for me and seventy-five cents for you to chop cotton. You have to keep up with me; so I'll show you how to chop fast when we get to the field. They might have a White man standing at the end of the cotton field watching us, and if you get far behind, they might not want to pay you. Sometimes they 'dock' your pay for the whole day if you're slow. I do not know that word "dock." Mother frowns when she says "dock," and I know it is a bad word.

Mother is frowning when she wakes me up. "I can't watch the baby in the field. I'll have to leave you home with the baby today. Go and clean up that bedroom!" she says. I get the broom and start sweeping the dirt out of the cracks and across the floor. The broom handle is up above my head, and I hold it in the middle and sweep the floor. A mouse runs out and turns the corner heading for the kitchen. "*Jeeeesssssssssuuuusssss! Lord, help me!*" Mother screams,

Man of the House

coming out of the kitchen. "*Get in there and kill that rat!*" she says. I go into the kitchen to look for the mouse. Just when I get to the kitchen door, I see the mouse standing still, right in the middle of the kitchen, looking up at me with two dark eyes.

I get down on the floor, and we look at each other. I can see it is breathing real hard and scared too. So, I whisper to the mouse, "You got to go out the back door, I tell you." It does not move.

"*What are you doing in there?!*" Mother yells at me.

"Talking to the mouse," I say.

"*Talking to that rat?!*" she screams. "*Kill that thing so I can get in there and cook!*" I wave my hand to get the mouse to go out of the back door before Mother catches me. I start to get up and the mouse runs around past me and back through the living room, and Mother screams again, "*Oh, Lord Jesus!*" and the mouse is gone. "Come here!" she yells. I go in to see her and she says, "When I tell you to do something, *you do what I say! I'm your mother*! You hear *me*?! Now go kill that rat like I told you to do!" I go into the bedroom where I first saw the mouse and find a hole in the floor underneath the bed near the wall. I don't know how I know but I go outside and under the house to look for the mouse. It is dark here, and I am crawling on my stomach, looking for the hole in the floor where the mouse had to come through to eat in the house.

I see the hole and lay still to rest. I can see a little in the dark now. The longer I stay here, the better I can see in the dark. I am looking for the mouse, and it knows because it is coming closer to me. Its nose is wiggling, and I see its bright eyes looking at me. It looks hungry. "I'm going in the house and get some bread for you, okay?" I say. Its nose wiggles, and I scoot on my stomach back out from under the house and sneak in the kitchen to steal some bread for it. I get a piece of old cornbread and rush back out and under the house to feed the mouse. It is still in the same place, and I crumble the cornbread and spread it out. The mouse is really hungry and eats fast. I hear Mother yelling for me to get back inside and clean the bedroom and help her cook. The mouse is still eating when I leave, and I want to bring it some water so it will not come back in the house to get it.

"Did you *kill* that rat?!" she yelled when I got back in the kitchen.

"I couldn't find it," I say.

Man of the House

"Are you telling me the truth?" she demands.

"Yes, ma'am," I lie.

"Get on that stool over there and start washing the dishes," she says, just when I start to go clean the bedroom.

I climb up on the stool near the dishpan and start washing dishes with the lye soap. "Jeeeessssssuuuuuuuussssssss!" Mother screams, running out of the kitchen, "Get something and *kill that rat like I told you!*"

I look down and the mouse is resting on its back legs, looking at me. I get down and give it water in a Coke bottle top real quick. Then I open the back door and make it go outside. "It's dead now," I lie again.

"*Praise the Lord,*" she said, coming back in the kitchen. "*It sure took you long enough to do what I told you to do!*" she says. I am scared now because the mouse might want more food and water. If Mother sees it again, she will beat me with the doubled extension cord. She starts putting the groceries away on the shelf, and the mouse comes back to the kitchen and stops at the door. Mother knows it's there. She can feel it. The mouse does not move. I am so scared now. Mother reaches for something and finds a Clorox bleach bottle. She slings it at the mouse and misses. The mouse screams, getting away, "Eeeeeeeeeeeeeee!" The top pops off the bottle and hits the mouse and wastes some on the floor. The mouse is gone, and Mother goes for her extension cord as I run for the bushes out in the backyard. "Get back *here!*" she yells at me.

I come back inside, and she beats me until I do not feel it. I just feel stinging all over and I am sore and bleeding on my legs and back. My back is stinging too. "Come outside with me. It's time for Mr. Wagner to come!" she says, walking to the front door. I am crying, and tears won't let me see. I go with her outside and wait with her till Mr. Wagner takes her away to the cottonfield. I am crying and hurting and stinging all over. I fall asleep and dream of the White girl and wake up sweating and scared. I wonder what it means to castrate a boy. I feel like I can hardly breathe. I am scared and worried about my dad. It is still dark outside, and I want to see lightning bugs flying in the air. I like seeing them. I remember now how angry Mother was about me looking at the White girl, and because I did not kill the mouse, I am double scared and worried about my dad and everything. It is dark when Mother comes back home, and my brothers and I keep real still on the floor, sitting against the wall, because when

Man of the House

I get up and walk, the shadows move on the wall and look like ghosts. Mother goes in the kitchen and eats, then she comes back to the bed in the living room and lies down and sleeps. I go outside and watch the lightning bugs and go back under the house. When I wake up, I sneak back inside of the house. Mother is standing in the kitchen doorway with her hands on her hips. *"Where have you been?!"* she yells. She whips out the extension cord and begins doubling it around her right fist and starts beating me with it. *"You had me worried half to death! Where have you been?"* Between the slashes, I tell her that I was scared about my dad and fell asleep under the house. *"Under the house?!"* she screams, and whops me as hard as she can with the doubled extension cord. "You don't go *anywhere* unless I say so, *do you hear me?!*" she screams.

"Yes, ma'am," I say, crying and running away from her and back outside.

Each morning she goes to work in the cottonfield and the babies cry inside of the house. I clean them, heat their milk, and feed both. Mother used to breastfeed Wil, and she started breast feeding Sav too, but he bit her nipple and made her scream. Now, saying, "This is my milk pump," she takes the bubble-looking breast pump and puts it against her left breast and squeezes the red part of it. Milk comes out of her breast and goes in the bottom of the glass part of the pump. Then she pours the milk in a big bottle and puts the bottle in the icebox to keep it fresh. One morning, she shows me how to take the big bottle out of the icebox, pour some in a pan, and put it on the stove to heat it, and then pour it in the baby bottle and feed him. I am still scared and worried about my dad. I make breakfast for myself and start cleaning the house. The mouse comes back in, and I feed it and put some water in the bottle cap for it. It has a white spot on its head from the bleach. I call him Spot and teach my brother to say Spot. We play with Spot all day until it gets almost dark outside and the lightning bugs are coming back out. Sometimes it is real dark when Mother gets home. I tell my brother that Mother will beat us if she sees the mouse. He laughs and says, "Spot! Spot!" He does not know what I mean about Mother, and he is only three years old, and Mother never beats him anyway. House flies are in the kitchen. They like the breadcrumbs on the table. I run to make them go outside and close the screen door with the big holes in it. Cockroaches are walking around in the kitchen too. They look like they are too old to run and must walk kinda slow, like that old man I saw in town.

Man of the House

NOTE: Senator Theodore G. Bilbo is NOT likely to be related to me. Instead, they wrote that " Your DNA matches provide evidence that you descend from James Edwin Bilbo (born 1822) and wife Louisa H. Jett, who married in Lawrence County, Mississippi in January 1846. They were enumerated in the following censuses, all of which list his main occupation as farmer:

- 1860 Lawrence County, Mississippi
- 1870 Marion County, Mississippi
- 1880 Washington Parish, Louisiana

Chapter 3
The Magic Words

> That which you see is not;
> and for that which is,
> you have no words.
> — Kabir

I want to go to kindergarten school, like Mother said. It is raining and thundering, then lightning when I wake up and see Mother sitting on the side of her bed. I hear the crickets singing. "Mother, how many crickets does it take to sing loud enough for us to hear them, even inside of the house?" I ask.

She smiles. "About a million," she says.

"How many is a million?" I ask.

"You know how to count to a hundred?" she says, and I say, "Yes." "Well," she says, "a million is one hundred times ten, and then it is one hundred times all of *that*!"

"Wow! How many is a thousand? I want to see a million crickets!" I say. "Can I go outside and see a million crickets!"

"Not now," she says. "And I'll tell you how many is a thousand when you finish washing those dishes and help me find something to feed your brothers." She takes the breast pump and says, "When I finish getting the milk out, you

Man of the House

get his bottle and pour some of this milk in it and feed him. I've got to nurse the new baby too."

She moves about, here and there, looking on shelves and checking the icebox for something to cook. "*Thank you, Jesus!*" she says, taking a box of grits off the shelf and a stick of margarine out of the icebox. "We'll just have to 'make-do' with what we've got," she says, smiling. "I already applied for welfare, and the social worker is a White woman, and she's gonna be coming here to find out if I am married and asking a lot of questions. I've gotta think of a story to tell her so she'll go away." Then, looking at me, she says, "When the White woman comes here, I want you to open the door and tell her I am sick, and I don't feel good. Now, remember, when you tell stories like this, you have to *concrete* your lies so you remember to say the same thing every time she asks questions! *You hear me?!* You got to *concrete* your lies, so you don't forget to tell her the same thing every time she comes here!"

There is a loud, crackling sound outside, and Mother calls me to get up and go outside with her to see if the sky is getting dark like it is going to rain. She pulls me with her outside to see what is happening. There is a rumbling sound of thunder, and then another rippling slash of lightning rips down the middle of the skies. "*Jesus!*" she whispers. "It sounds like the lightning struck a tree or something just down the road. Let's get back inside. Quick!" she says. "What time is it?" She looks at the black Big Bend clock on the head of her bed and says "Lord, Lord. Put out the lamp!" The thunder roars, and more lightning flashes across the skies. It seems that the lightning might have hit something, and inside of the house it is getting dark. "Let's *pray*," Mother says in a shaking voice. I know she is really scared of lightning; but I do not know what to say to God. She prays, and I listen. Lightning flashes, and I see Mother's face. "Come over here by me," she says, and I scoot across the floor and sit beside her. Thunder is rumbling across the heavens, and more lightning strikes. It seems to cut through something, and the rain begins pounding the tin roof of our house. "*Lord, have mercy!*" Mother prays. The rain is falling heavier, and the wind is shaking the house. The storm rages, and Mother says something about the "ship at sea" and "peace be still." The wind is whistling around corners, and a tree branch falls in the front yard and on the front porch. "It's a thunderstorm," Mother says. Soon we

Man of the House

can even hear water running across the yard. I can hear water running in the ditch in front of the house, too. The frogs begin croaking louder and the crickets stop singing. "Go check on the babies and *get back here*!" she said.

I like the rain, and I know Mother is scared. The house is cool now. We have one window in the living room and one in the kitchen. We must open the windows to let air in the house because it is hot. The babies are still sleeping, and I come back and sit next to Mother. A gust of wind shakes the house again and Mother says, "*Lord, have mercy on us!*" There is another loud "thud" sound on the roof, like a tree limb fell on it. "*Lord, Lord, Lord,*" Mother cries. "I know I'm not going to be able to go to the field with this much rain," she says. I am happy.

"Can I go to school?" I ask.

"Do you know we do not have any food in the kitchen?" she says.

"Yes, ma'am," I answer.

"You can't go to school on an *empty stomach*! I hear what you're *thinking*," she says. Lightning flashes brighten the room as the rain pounds the roof and the wind threatens to move our house somewhere else. Mother keeps praying, and I start wondering what I will have to do if I cannot go to school. Lightning flashes through our window and lights up the room. "*Please, Jesus!*" Mother cries. The wind whistles around the corners of the house and shakes it. Mother lowers her head in prayer. "Are you sure the babies are okay?" she asks. I say yes as something falls on the front porch like a big rock. "Oh, *Lord*," Mother says. I go to the door to check on the big thud. "Be careful opening that door!" she says as I walk out onto the porch and see the tree limb. A streak of lightning rips across the blue-black skies and lights up the whole world. I want to sit outside and watch the sky change colors.

"Mother," I start.

"*Get back in here!*" she yells. I want to tell her how beautiful the sky is. It is a long time before the storm ends, and we go back to bed. Mother says, "I know Mr. Wagner is not going to the field. Lord, I don't know *what we're going to do about food*. Go get some sleep," she tells me, and I get in bed with the others in the bedroom. Mother sleeps in the living room.

She takes me to my first kindergarten class at the St. Andrews M. B. Church the next day. She holds my right hand as we walk up the steps to the front of the church. I pull my hand out of Mother's hand and crawl up the steps to the top and run to the front doors where my teacher, Mrs. White, is standing and smiling. I see an open door to the left and run in it. Mother reaches for me and begins yelling for me to get back to her; and just then, Mrs. White quietly says, "Let him go." I look back and see Mrs. White smiling softly. Just inside, I see lots of things on shelves and a sandbox, two kiddie chairs, and lots of real toys. At home we only had tiny plastic toys from the Cracker Jack boxes. I sit in one of the chairs and begin looking around the little room with all of the things put together on shelves. Those things are all around the room. The box of sand is close to the wall with yellow ducks in it. Mrs. White comes into the room and gets down on her knees close to the other kiddie chair. She smiles and takes one of the things off the shelf and asks me if I want to learn how to read.

I say, "Yes, ma'am," and I do not know what a read is.

She takes one of the things off the shelf with ducks on the front, like the ones in the sandbox, and says, "This is a 'book,'" and I look on the front of it at the picture of ducks. She says that their names are Mr. and Mrs. Donald Duck and that the little ones are kids like me. Mrs. White reads to me from the book and teaches me how to take care of the ducks in the sandbox. She goes back inside of the church to check on the other kids and then comes back and begins teaching me my alphabets. I pick up the Donald Duck book and hold it while watching her pick out alphabets and call them different names.

She takes one of the alphabet things and pulls it slowly up close to another alphabet thing, and then she pulls another one close to those and calls them a word. She tells me the "word's" name and helps me to make a word like she did. She moves the alphabets away from each other and makes them into other words, and names them each time. Then she makes more and more words and calls them a sentence. I am feeling things change in my whole body, and I want to make sentences, too, like she does. She looks at me looking at the new thing she called a sentence. Then she touches my right hand with her finger and says, "You can make a sentence if you want to." My heart is beating real fast now, and it is like being with lightning bugs and seeing how they make the night more fun when they get close to me and sparkle their lights. One day, Mrs. White takes the alphabets and makes words and sentences, and then she makes something new and calls it a paragraph and asks me to "read" it. Inside, my body turns black. I do not know what "read" is, and I am scared to make a mistake. Mother whips me with the double extension cord when I make mistakes. Maybe Mrs. White will beat me too.

She touches my hand and sits closer to me. I feel warm inside again. "Do you want to read?" she asks. She says the paragraph and says, "See how I read the paragraph? You can do it too." Now I know what "read" means, and I start reading words and sentences and the paragraph thing. Sometimes she shows me how to count, too, with the numbers things, just like she did with the alphabets things. The whole big world is bigger and bigger and bigger in this room, and I am inside of the big, big, big world now.

Every day Mother lets me walk to the church and play with the ducks, and Mrs. White is always at the front door. Now she tells me to come up front and sit with the other kids, and we sing, "Jesus loves me, this I know because the Bible tells me so." Then I run back to the little room and get the Donald Duck book and sit in the sandbox till she comes in and starts teaching me the alphabets and how to put letters together to make words. She reads to me and tells me to read what she is reading. She moves her finger real slow along the line she is reading. Sometimes she tells me about the letters in a word and the colors in the book, and sometimes she teaches me numbers. Lots of time passes, and she starts telling me to read to her. She helps me when I do not know a word. Soon I can read the Donald Duck book and play with the little ducks in the sandbox because I know their names now. She says the ducks are a family, and I know my alphabets now and I can count to a hundred. At home, Mother helps me to learn how to count up to a thousand and read Tar Baby and the little old lady who lives in a shoe who has so many children that she doesn't know what to do. Mrs. White helps me to make words and learn to read.

One Easter Sunday, Mother takes me to the St. Andrews Church with her. We leave our house and start walking toward Ms. Mullen's Store, and I see other ladies in big hats walking slowly across the road in front of us. Other adults are walking slow, talking, and laughing, going to the church. All of the adult ladies have bags in their hands too. When we get to the church, Mother points to an old lady bending down to the ground and tells me to go and help her to hide her Easter eggs because she cannot get down on her knees to put the eggs in the grass and hide them. The lady gives the sack of eggs to me to hide and smiles when she walks on to the church. When it is time for us to go and search for Easter eggs, I know where to find a lot of them, and I run back with the sack the lady gave me and get as many as I can for our house because we did not have any food to eat. Mama, Mother's mother, cooks in the White school's cafeteria, and some days she brings us pint boxes of chocolate and white milk, small bowls of carrot salad, a loaf of Wonder Bread, and rolls of toilet tissue.

I run and climb on the front porch and run and jump off on the ground. My right leg is hurting, and I hold it, sitting on the ground. "What's wrong with you!?" Mother yells and comes and helps me up. It hurts to walk, and she takes me to see Dr. Hood in Mound Bayou. We get out of the car and a big bird starts walking to meet us. It has a long neck and lots of feathers going all the way down to the ground. "That's a peacock," Mother says. "Look how many colors it has! See the long blue feathers!" The sun is shining, and the bird, I mean the peacock is walking slow to meet us and we are getting close to it. Little feathers are sticking up on its head. I am not hurting now. I want my hand out of Mother's hand so I can go play with the peacock. Everything goes away and only the peacock is here. Everything is green and blue, and it is quiet. "LET'S GET INSIDE TO SEE DR. HOOD!" Mother yells. I see the peacock again and look back as Mother pulls me away to the hospital door. When we get inside the big room with chairs around the sides of it, I look straight in front of me and see a green bird. We get close to the bird in the cage, and it says, "Hi, little boy!"

I stop and stare in its dark eyes, and we look at each other. "Come on, now!" Mother says and pulls me away from the green bird.

Some ladies in white dresses put me on a table and start doing lots of things. I see Dr. Hood coming in the room smiling. When I wake up, Dr. Hood is standing next to me, talking to Mother, and we soon go back home. I have a long white thing on my right leg, and Mother calls it a cast and tells me that my right leg is broken so I will have to stay in bed for a long time. She takes me to Mama's house and on into the kitchen and helps me get into the small bed. She goes back in the front room, and I fall back to sleep till Mama comes and wakes me up and gives me food to eat. *Don't move!* I'll have to feed

Man of the House

you," Mama says. "Your mother had to go home and take care of the other children. You're going to stay here with me till you get well. You've gone and broken your leg and now your mother must do all of the work taking care of the babies and working and everything all by herself! And *I have to work, too*, and I'll feed you before I go to work and leave something for you to eat by the bed till I get back home. See what you've done to your poor mother and me! Thank the Lord tomorrow is Friday and I'll be home after that to take care of you!"

It is dark when I wake up, and my penis is hard. I start playing with it and Mama comes in the kitchen, hollering, "*What are you doing?! You little nasty thing*! Get back to sleep and don't make me have to come back in here again!" The sun is shining in the kitchen when Mama comes in and gives me breakfast and helps me get out of bed and into the front room with her. She has a big bed and says that she needs her double mattress on it so her back will not hurt. The front window is big, too, and her Singer's sewing machine is right in front of it with lots of pieces of cloth and different colors of thread on tiny spools. "I'm going to make you a suit to wear one day," she says. I want a suit and I am really happy now. My own suit! And Mama is going to make it just for me! She brings her two straw-bottom chairs near the fireplace and helps me to sit in the one next to her big brown piano. She has a big window next to the piano and I can see Cree and Chloe's house next to her house. "I've got to get my snuff and green stamps," she says, moving around behind me. Then she sits in the other chair, opens the snuff can and shakes snuff in the top, puts the can down and pulls her lower lip open, shakes the snuff down in it, waves her hand before her face to make the dust go away, and closes the can. "Now, I am going to show you how to help me do the green stamps so I can buy a blanket for the bed," she says, getting a book and opening it. The pages are blank with tiny squares all over them. "See, watch me," she starts, squirting a long streak of snuff juice through her top front teeth straight into the fire burning two logs in the fireplace. "Sreeeeeeee," the fire says, and Mama looks down at the open book, licks a green stamp, and sticks it on one of the squares in the book. She shoots another long streak of snuff juice on the fire, and it cries again.

"Okay, you get another book like mine and do what you see me doing," she says. I do not have any snuff and I better not ask her for some of her snuff 'cause she says it is for grown folks. I want to squirt snuff juice, too. I start doing the green stamps like she is doing, and they taste nasty. "One day I am going to take you to Mrs. White's house and ask her to teach you how to play the piano for me," she says, squirting another streak of snuff juice on the crying fire, and it stops burning the logs in that spot for a little while, then it burns in that spot again. I look at the thing on a table next to the door going into the kitchen and ask her what it is. "That's my telephone," she says, "and don't pick it up, because somebody might be on the line, and you're not supposed to be listening when grown folks are talking. Oh, I forgot to turn on the light and it's getting dark in here." She gets up and goes to the middle of the room, pulls the white string hanging from the ceiling, and a light comes on and makes the room real bright. Mother does not have a light in our house, and we use a kerosene lamp. And Mama has a refrigerator, too, and Mother has an icebox and buys ice from the ice man.

The house is quiet, and I do not smell baby poop and pee. Mother comes, and Mama tells her how she is teaching me to do green stamps and that she is going to make me a suit and get Ms. White to teach me how to play the piano for her. Mother smiles and goes into the kitchen behind Mama. I look at the shelf over the fireplace, and the piano with the white and black fingers on it. Mama says the fingers are *keys* that make music come out of the piano. They come back out of the kitchen. Mother says "Yes, ma'am" to her and looks at me, smiling, and says, "We're going to move soon." Then she leaves through the front room door with a bag in her hands.

"I gave her some food for the children," Mama tells me, "Now, how many pages have you filled with green stamps?"

I say, "All these," showing her my book, and keep licking and putting the green stamps on the empty blocks in the book. She squirts a shot of snuff juice on the crying fire again and it goes out in that spot, then it comes back up.

NOTE: I have contracted with Ancestry.com to obtain their expert help in tracing my relationship, if any, with Senator Theodore G. Bilbo and any other close relationships I may have.

Chapter 4
Sexual Abuse

The savior I had imagined for so long was a phony.
I felt more angry at him than I did at Mother.
I wished that somehow I could fly away,
but the throbbing pain brought me back to reality.
— Dave Pelzer

One day soon, Mother comes to take me back to see Dr. Hood and he takes the cast off my leg. I do not see the peacock today, and the green bird says "Hi, little boy" again, but Mother will not let me stay and talk to it. The man is waiting in the car to take us back home, and we have to hurry, she says. We get home, and Mother says I have to be really careful so I do not break my leg again and she will let me go back to school till my leg gets well. I go to the big school to start the first grade, and the new teacher tells us about our books and says we are going to learn how to count. I sit in the front row, and she starts talking about the books we are going to read. I raise my hand and tell her about Mrs. White and how I can read the book in her hand. She says to come to her desk and show her how I can read. She smiles and takes me with her to the principal's office and gets me promoted to second grade. On my first day in the second grade, I meet the twin girls who lived next door to Mama, and their names are Cree and Chloe. I like Cree, and she likes me, too. I sit with them, and we talk about lots of things all day; then we run together to Mama's house. When we get to the back of Mama's house, Cree yells, "Let's play Mama and Daddy!" and I say, "OKAY!" Mama's house is raised about two feet off the ground on concrete blocks and we run underneath her house, take our clothes off, and start playing Daddy and Mama. Chloe sits on the right side and watches us.

Suddenly we hear Mama screaming, *"Get your nasty self off that nice little girl*! Go and get me three switches! Braid them and bring them here so I can whip you!" The girls run home next door, and Mama beats me until the switch shreds into splinters. "Get up and go inside and clean your *nasty self*!" she yells, breathlessly, as she pants and wipes sweat from her face. She comes inside yelling, "You little nasty thing! Look how you *forced* me to stop and beat you when I am already tired from working all day!" After taking a bath and getting back in my clothes, Mama is relaxed a bit and tells me to come with her so she can tell Mother what a nasty little thing I have become, and she'll make Mother beat some sense into me. She catches me by the collar of my shirt and pulls me out of the door and tells me to walk on the left side of her because boys are never supposed to allow cars to splash dirt and water on ladies. Once back home, she tells Mother everything she saw me doing with Cree and tells Mother that she needs to beat me again for being so nasty and making her have to leave home and bring me back. Mother looks at me with a smirk on her face and gets the six-foot extension cord, doubles it, and beats me again, and tells me that she is whipping me for peeing in the bed the night before, too. I bolt and run away from her. "I didn't forget you wet the bed!" Night comes and I have to put my siblings to bed; then Mother tells me to take off my shirt and pants and say *The Lord's Prayer* with my eyes closed. I begin praying and she walks quietly into the room and beats me with the doubled extension cord again, saying, "*I got you now*!" She beats me across my naked back and the cord stings with pain.

One morning Mama knocks and walks in the house and says to Mother, "Your Aunt Susie and Uncle Buck are coming for dinner today. You should bring the kids so they can play with the others."

Mother says, "Yes, ma'am," and Mama walks back out. She is cooking when we get there, and I start playing with Cha Cha and her sister.

Man of the House

"Keep the kids outside," Mama tells Mother.

"Yes, ma'am." Looking at us standing at the front door, Mother says, "Stay outside in the yard and play!"

We turn around and go back in the yard and play hide-and-seek. "Do you know how to make mud-cakes?" I ask Cha Cha.

"Yea!" she says. "Wanna make sum?"

"Yeah!" We sit on the ground and stir some mud and make biscuits. Then we put them in the sunlight so they can cook. I hear Mama saying to Mother: "Leslie! *Are you pregnant again*?!" We listen to the grown folks talking.

"Yes, ma'am. *It was a mistake, Mama*," she says. "I didn't plan on it."

It is late in the afternoon when Mother comes to the screen door and yells at us, "Okay, come inside and eat!" All of the grown folks go into the living room after they eat, and now we can eat. We have turnip greens, cornbread, and some meat. When Mama gets home from cooking at the White school, she brings white and chocolate milk, Wonder Bread, rolls of toilet paper, and carrot salad home. I want some chocolate milk to drink, and Mother says no, and that we must eat quickly because Uncle Buck and Aunt Susie will have to drive all the way back to Greenville. When they leave in the big Ford car, Mother takes us back home. I like playing on the ground and go to the back yard and sit on the grass. I see a small snail and it stops right in front of me. It moves really slow and has two tiny things sticking up on its head. It is moving, and the sunlight shines over its soft and glossy skin. I lie down on the ground and stretch out on my stomach in front of the little snail and watch it move. It stops right in front of my face and . . . "*What are you doing*?!" Mother screams at me. "*Get away from that nasty thing*!" I look up at her as she turns back into the house and start getting up and moving back. My heart beats from her screaming. I am scared. Mother comes back to the door and begins pouring salt on the snail. Its whole body is twisting and twisting. Mother laughs and says, "*Now! That nasty thing is dead*! Get up and clean yourself and go check on the babies!" I am looking back at the place where the snail *used to be*.

All of the babies are sleeping, and I go out the front door and lay on the grass near the Willow tree and look for four-leaf clovers for a while. I find one and flip over on my back and watch the clouds move. Way, way, up in the sky I see a plane moving real slow, and white cloud-looking stuff is coming out of its tail and spreading out. Maybe it is making clouds… I want to fly an airplane when I grow up, and I can go up there and make clouds too. Suddenly, Mother is standing behind my head. "What are you doing?" she asks.

"I want to fly an airplane when I grow up," I tell her.

"You know *the White folks are not going to let you fly an airplane*! Get up off that dirt and dust yourself off!" she says. "Haven't you *got something to do* in the house?!"

When the next morning comes, it is raining, lightning, and thundering. Mother says I cannot go to school today. I walk to the corner and see the school down the street from Ms. Mullen's Store on the corner. I see some other kids running around in the school yard down the road. When I get back home, I see that the gray dirt in the yard has turned into black mud, and big puddles of water hang in spots across the yard. Our weeping willow tree near the ditch hangs down into the rushing water. A lot of the tree's leaves are muddy, wet, and flowing in the water. A few black birds are hopping about catching earthworms that come out of the ground. One bird has a long earthwork in its mouth, just wiggling and hanging from both sides, and the bird looks at me, then flies up into another tree and eats the worm. Muddy water rushes down the ditch in front of our house and splashes against the wood plank going from our yard to the gravel road. It is quiet everywhere now.

One day Mother takes me to Ms. Bonnie's house so she can babysit me. It is almost daylight. She tells me that Ms. Bonnie is fourteen years old and she will be babysitting another boy, named Diff, too. Mother and Ms. Bonnie smile when she walks away and leaves me. "Come mon wid me," Ms. Bonnie whispers, looking down at me. I follow her into the kitchen. She takes off her clothes, standing in front of me, and says, "Take yo clothes off! Come mon, do lak me! Take yo clothes off! Um mon show you how-tur-do it! Come mon!" I look at all the hair between her legs and I am scared. She reaches up and jerks my clothes off, pulls me down on top of her, and says, "Put it in! Put it in! Come mon, put it in lak I tol you!" I don't know what to put in where. "Um gon tell!" Diff screams through the side window. Ms. Bonnie pushes me up a little, pulls my penis, and tells me again, "Put it in!" Just then Mama shoves open the front door and yells, "Get your little nasty self off that nice lady and come home with me! Get home! I'm going to beat the hide off you for messing

Man of the House

with that nice lady when she is just trying to take care of you! *You filthy little thing*!" When we get to Mama's house, she tells me to get three switches from the bush in her front yard, braid them, and bring it to her so she can whip me. I do this, and she orders me to take off my shirt and lie on the ground in front of her. I do. She beats me across the back until the switch splinters into fine little pieces on the ground. "Get up!" she demands. "And get in the house and wash your little nasty self!" I do this. "Now, I'm gonna take you home to your mother," she declares, "and make her beat you again for messing with that nice lady and making me waste my time whipping you, and you know I got to go to work in the White folks' kitchen. They might think I am late getting to work! Look at what *you made me do*! Get your clothes on so I can take you to your mother!" She takes me home and orders Mother to beat me for messing with that nice lady. Mother beats me again with her six-foot extension cord, doubled, and with the plug-end gripped in her right hand.

Chapter 5
The Good and the Bad

> There is a Secret One inside us;
> the planets in all the galaxies
> pass through Her hands like beads.
> — Kabir

Soon we move next door to my godparents—Jeff and Bliss Aston. My godfather comes to our house and plays with Mother. She lets me go see godmother, who takes down the large cloth handbag with the long shoulder straps filled with the different parts of a thousand-piece puzzle. It hangs on the right-side wall in her dining room behind the table. Each time I visit her, she takes me by the hand and, smiling, escorts me to the dining room, takes down the large handbag of puzzle pieces, and softly whispers to me: "If you find two pieces that fit together, *I will kiss you!*" My godmother's home is clean and smells nice, too. It is quiet in here. She takes the puzzles off the wall and empties the bag of its pieces on the floor, smiles at me, and walks away into the kitchen. The whole room is mine now, and before me lay so many tiny pieces of a puzzle.

No one has ever kissed me, and I lie here taking one piece of the puzzle in one hand and bringing another piece up to it to see if it will fit. I keep doing this for a long time. Hours pass, and she comes to tell me that I have to go home for the night and that she will not let anyone touch the puzzle pieces while I am gone. She walks me to the door, touches my shoulder, and says, "Good night." Evening after evening I run to her house after Mother comes home from chopping or picking cotton. And just as she promised, each day I find the puzzle pieces where I had left them. I always scan the puzzle pieces before to see where I left off the day before. Every piece of the puzzle is different, and I am scared because if one piece goes into the other one just right, I do not know what people do when they kiss.

> The price we pay for…willful ignorance is
> our massive achievement gaps [in education].
> It is too high. —Lisa Hansel

The Peacock Lady. My godmother's image, clothed in the memory of the blue indigo peacock who walked about the grounds of the Truth Hospital. Dr. Hood brought the peacock to the hospital. **Commissioned artwork created by Dr. Caroline (Kay) Picart.**

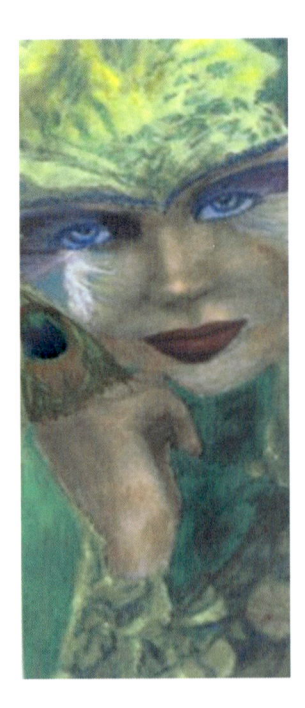

Man of the House

*Love is the way messengers
from the mystery tell us things.*

*Love...shines inside us,
visible-invisible, as we trust
or lose trust, or feel it start to grow again.*
— Rumi

Nobody has ever kissed me. Mother just tells me what to do and how to do things. Daddy is gone, and Mother says he is not coming back. And Mama (Mother's mother) beats me a lot when she is mad. I get one piece of the puzzle and ease it close to the one in my other hand. I want it to fit, and I am scared 'cause I want Godmother to kiss me. I do not hear her when she comes in the room and, as before, says, "You have to go home now. It is real dark outside. I will let everything stay right where it is until you come back, okay?" On a Sunday afternoon, I run to my godmother's home and go straight to the scattered pieces of puzzle on the dining room floor. They are all there where I left them, and I lie on one side as I gently test one piece after another in search of the two pieces that fit. The afternoon grows into early evening as the one piece slips into the other! My heart beats real fast, and I am scared she might say, "No. It does not fit." I cannot feel myself breathing. I check the two pieces in the middle of my right hand. The fit is a little bit tight, and I get up real slow and walk into the living room where she sits in her rocking chair, smiling and reaching out to me with both hands open as she says, "Put them in my hands, honey." I do, and she looks at the pieces. Then she comes out of her chair so quick and she is on her knees in front of me. Her bright dark brown eyes are so close; she draws me into her arms and holds me so tightly that I feel only her warm body and my face getting wet. Her tears are on my face, and she kisses me. I reach up and put my hands on her shoulders. I feel warm and happy, and I am crying, too. Then she slowly moves back and away from me. I do not want her to move away. She kisses my right cheek again and says, "*This is beautiful*! You did good. You did so *very good*!" Then she wipes her face dry and wipes my face and eyes. I see her face covered in tiny little freckles. I stare at her freckles, and I want to count them one by one, like I did with the puzzle pieces. Then she says, "You will have to go home now," and she gets up and walks me to the front door. I walk out into the dark night and go back in our house.

My godfather knocks on our door the next morning, and I open the door. Mother rushes to the door, smiling, and pushes me back. He whispers to Mother, and they look down at the floor. Then he leaves and Mother closes the door, and, looking at me, she says, "Your godmother died!" I run to my godmother's house and the front door is locked. I cannot get in. I go back home, and Mother meets me at the door and says, "The funeral home people are going to get her." I ask if I can go to my godmother's funeral, and she says, "NO!" A big black car backs up close to Godmother's front door and stops. I am standing on our front porch when two men come out of her house with something long and it is covered over. One man walks backward toward the back of the big car, and the other man, at the back of the long-covered thing, talks to him until they get close to the back of the car. The man at the front of the long thing turns around and takes one hand to open the back of the car and puts the long thing down in the car and the other man pushes it all the way in the car. They get in the car and drive away.

I take care of my brothers when Mother goes to work in the cottonfields every day. On Saturdays, she comes home in the evening and makes me clean the house and wash diapers because she is tired. She says that Sunday is the Lord's Day, and she cannot work because Sunday is sacred. She tells me that it took God six days and nights to create the earth and everything in it, and then He was tired and rested on Sunday. That's why Sunday is sacred. Every Sunday, and at night too, Mother is very tired like God was tired. She says that's why she taught me how to iron clothes, change and wash baby diapers, feed and watch them so they do not put just anything in their mouths. She needs to rest to get ready to go to work Monday mornings. I am the Man of the House too, she says. So, I have to watch out for my brothers, so they do not run out in the gravel road and get hurt, and I have to light the kerosene lamp when it is dark, so they don't get scared of the dark.

It is very dark outside now, and Mother is not home. All three of us are sitting on the floor listening to the crickets outside, when we hear a lot of loud laughing and a man talking, and then the front door swings open and Mother

Man of the House

comes in with a man holding her. They are laughing so hard that Mother's face is wet with tears. They are holding each other and wandering over to the bed and ripping each other's clothes off. The man gets on top of Mother and they are having a lot of fun. She opens her legs, and the man reaches between his legs and lies back down on top of her. They look like they are fighting, and I am scared. The man groans, and Mother prays. Then they stop fighting and lie together on the bed and sleep.

Two of my siblings start school, and Mother tells me to help each one with his homework. I have three brothers now and one is a baby. Mother takes me with her to pick blackberries so she can make a pie. The blackberries are on long vines hanging over the ditch, and she says Mrs. Mullen will pay me for empty cans and soda bottles too. The vines scratch me when I go between them to get the blackberries, and she holds the bucket. "Don't let the thorns stick you," she says, and they keep sticking me. "Push the vines open! Yes, like that, and get all the black ones!" One vine falls over my neck when I am getting the berry down at the bottom and it sticks and makes my neck bleed. "Hurry," Mother says, "it's getting dark!" I hurry to pick the berries and the thorns keep sticking me. Little blood spots are on my hands and neck. I see an empty bottle and get it too. We get back home, and she gives me the sack I got from the lady at church long time ago when I hid the Easter eggs and tells me to use it when I look for empty bottles and cans. The kitchen smells good while she is cooking the blackberry pie and my stomach is growling. I am on my knees in one of the chairs in the kitchen watching her cook the pie. Mother tastes everything while she cooks, and now she says she is not hungry anymore and lets me eat the leftover blackberries. My stomach stops growling. "Go check on the babies," she says. I have to change Sav's diaper using the safety pin, and it is hard to get it to go through the diaper on the right side. I push real hard, and he cries. I pull it out so I can see what makes it so hard to go through the diaper. Now I am scared because I pushed the safety pin through his skin. I have to get him to hush before Mother finds out what I did and beats me. I put my finger under the diaper and get it fastened, fasten the other side, and take him outdoors to play till he stops crying.

Barry is the new baby, and his poop diapers are not like Yalla's diapers used to be with the yellow poop that ran down his legs a lot. Mother says that the stork forgot to bring his sister two years ago and now she has six boys, and she keeps praying to God to have a baby girl so she will have someone to talk to about girl things. "One day," she says, "all these boys will grow up and *takeover my house*! I've got to get a man in here *to make these boys obey*! But *no man's* gonna want a woman with six boys in the house! I feel like the little ol' lady that lived in a shoe and had so many children she didn't know what to do! Lord, I don't wanna get married, though. *That's like going to jail*!" She keeps talking to herself, doing lots of things in the kitchen, and rushing in and out of the other two rooms in the house. "I smell something!" she cries with a smirk on her face. "Go check on that night can and take it out back and dump it if it's got boo-boo in it," she says to me. We use a Folgers Coffee can at night to poop and pee, and in the mornings, I have to take it out far in the back yard and empty and clean it and bring it back in the house.

I help Will and Zarv with their homework, and it is getting too dark in the house for me to read my books. When I go out to pick blackberries for Mother, I take my Easter egg sack for cans and bottles. The thorns on the blackberry vines stick me a lot, and sometimes I find lots of bottles and cans too and take them to Mrs. Mullen's store. One day when I go to her store, I see a long red thing and ask what it is. She says it's a flashlight and shows me how to use it to make light, and I want it to read at night, and she tells me how many cans and bottles I need to buy it. When I tell Mother about it, she says I can get busy looking for cans and bottles to get it and help my brothers to do their homework. Now I go everywhere Black people can go in town and look for empty cans and bottles till I get enough, and Mrs. Mullen sells me the flashlight and tells me I will need more cans and bottles when the batteries die. I have to get two batteries to make the flashlight make light. I help Will and Zavr with their homework and read my books now, and when it starts getting dark, I use the flashlight. Mother says I cannot read all night because a little knowledge is dangerous and too much will kill me, and don't start getting curious because curiosity killed the cat.

We start reading one afternoon and Mother whispers, running into the kitchen, "Look," she says to me, "see that car out front with the White lady getting out?!"

I say, "Yes, ma'am," and she whispers, "That's the Welfare Lady! Go to the door and tell her I am sick and I cannot come to the door! Remember to concrete your lies 'cause she'll come back again to see if I am married and cut me off welfare!" She goes in the kitchen and on out back of the house. I open the front door and the lady is smiling and walking to the house. "Where's your mother, honey?" she asks, and I tell her, "Mother is sick and she cannot come to see you now."

She says, "Well, I hope your Mommy gets well soon. Tell her I just stopped by to see how she's doing." My heart is beating real fast, and the lady gets back in her black car and goes away. Mother comes back inside, wiping sweat off her face, saying "Wheee-ooh! That was close. What would have happened if I had not been walking through the house and *spotted her through the window!? Lord Jesus! We'd lose our commodities!* We only get two boxes of cheese, four sticks of butter, four boxes of dried eggs, four boxes of powdered milk, and . . . Lord, that's all we get for a whole month, and I've got six mouths to feed. *Lord, I don't know what to do!*"

It gets dark soon and I have to sneak and read my books. Mother lets me go looking for empty bottles and cans, and picking blackberries, and sometimes it is dark when I get back home. Now I can hide underneath the house or behind St. Andrew's Church and read my books with a flashlight. I am eight years old now, and Mother wakes me early one morning and tells me to get dressed, wake up the other kids, and make sure they are all bathed, clothed, fed, and ready for school. She goes outside in the garden. I have five brothers now, and I am the oldest. Three are still wearing diapers, and one has almost learned to use the potty on his own. Two can go to school, and I must stay home and take care of the others while Mother works in the cottonfield. Then one day when it is real dark, I light the kerosene lamp and we sit on the floor around the walls and watch the shadows of the lamp's flame flicker against the walls. Mother has said that ghosts will come in through the walls and doors to get us if we do bad things while she is gone.

Suddenly there is a thunderously loud bang against the front door, and it pops open! An ashen-faced Black man wearing dirt-covered overalls, a dirt-stained hat, and dirt-covered shoes stands in the doorway with bead-like eyes and tobacco-stained flat teeth. I jump up nervously and start toward the door. I see Mother standing behind him. I glance around and see all the other kids crunched against the walls. The man's face is covered in cotton-picker's dirt, and his sharp flat teeth are gritted against each other. His bead-like, tiny brown

Man of the House

eyes are cold and threatening. He barks, "Who de one thanks he de *Main ur de House?* Who dat thank he de Main in de House?!" I stand there looking up at him. My knees trembling and my heart beats real fast. Looking down at me, he says, "Dat muss be yu, since you, thank you grown 'n-sich!" Mother stands behind him and I want her to say something to get the stranger out of our home. She looks down on the floor. "Um gon show you who de Main uv dis house, *you Black Sapsucker*! Um yo' nu Daddy! Um yo' nu Daddy, *nig-gur*!" The dark, little, black ashen-faced man wearing the dirt-stained overalls with the gritted tobacco-stained teeth kicks me in my stomach and I reel across the floor and against the wall. "Um ma teech chu who de Main ur de house!" he bellows. "Me 'n ya Mama don't got marred, *Sucker*! *Us got marred by oughts*! You know what *'oughts'* is?! Dat mean *chullun oughts tur keeps de goawddamn moufs shet!* Na, shet cho fukkin'mouff, nig-gur! You cryin' na, 'n I ain't ebben got started kicking yo Black nasty azz yit! Git up offen dat flo 'n dry yo fukkin' eyes nig-gur fo I kick yo azz ur-gin!" No one had ever called me a "nigger" before, but since he is looking at me, I know that is my new name. I start up from the floor, and he kicks me again in my stomach. I am trying real hard to breathe. I hold myself up by leaning against the wall. I am trying to breathe. I look at Mother from the corner of my eyes and I see a smirk on her face.

The strange man spins around and rushes back outside. Within minutes he comes rushing back inside of the house with a long stick, and raising it back over his head, he yells, "Um gon beat yo' Black azz wif dis har stick 'n teech chu who de Main uv de hase!" I run for the front door, pushing past Mother, and jump off the front porch, landing atop a tree stump. My right foot slides off the right side of the stump, and my left foot hits the ground. The round corner of the tree stump strikes me between my legs, and the night turns black with flickering stars.

I wake up in the Truth Hospital in Mound Bayou, hearing Dr. Hood ask Mother, "What happened to this boy? His right testicle has been severely damaged and probably will not grow anymore, but the left side is fine. He has a hernia. It could be painful if he lifts anything heavy. You will need to lay him down if the hernia starts to swell. Do not let him lift anything heavier than five pounds." Mother nods her head and tells Dr. Hood that she does not know what happened to me. Her new man stares at the floor, shuffling his feet and scratching his head feverishly. Again, Dr. Hood asks Mother how this happened?

Man of the House

She drops her head and says, "I don't know."

Dr. Hood says that he will not do surgery and tells Mother again, "Give him plenty of rest if the hernia flares up." I hear the word "rest" and I know now that I might get a chance to go back to school if I do not have to lift anything. I have been out of school for a long time. Maybe I will not know anything when I get back in school. I am worried that my teachers might ask me a question and I will not know what to say.

On the first day back in school, I can pray that my teacher will not ask me any questions. I get by, and after returning home I sit near the fireplace and begin reading a book. Mother's new man stares at me and thunders, "Whut chu doin wid dat gauddamn buk? Yu thank um ur fool?! I ben tur skool! I went in de frunt do, pissed up ginst de wall, n waulked out de bak do'! I ain't no fool! I ben tur skool! Ni, yu git yo stankin' Black azz offend at flo, n don't let me ketch you niggar azz settin' round' har studdin' no buk no mo! You harr me, *nig-gar*?!" I look down on the floor because Mother says I am supposed to look on the floor when grown folks talk to me. "*You sa Ya, sur*, wen I talks tur you, *nig-gar*!"

I say, "Yes, sir," and leave the room to hide my book. Every morning now I get ready to go to the cottonfields. First, Mother tells me that her new man's name is Hardface, and we will have to move to Duncan so he can see his mother.

The next morning, we are taken to his mother's house, and Mother says her name is Ms. Kuss. We all get out of Hardface's green 1949 Pontiac and go inside the house. Ms. Kuss is sitting in a straw-bottomed chair. She has her right foot on the floor and her left leg has been cut off at the knee. Mother whispers that she is diabetic, and the doctors had to remove her left leg. The fireplace is in front of her and lots of old clothes are piled up on the floor and sofa. I see a door opening to the kitchen. The house smells really bad. Ms. Kuss looks slowly around and turns up her nose and says, "Whut chu brang dem gowddamned chaps in my house fur? Git me dat dare needle n medicine so's I kin give mysef ur shot!" Hardface runs to get the needle and medicine and gives it to her. She raises her dress and sticks the needle in her thigh, then yells, "Git dem goaddamned chaps outter my house!" Mother tells me to take my siblings outside and wait for them near the car.

Man of the House

We move to a house in Hushpuckena. Hardface drives three miles down gravel roads before getting to the house we are moving into. We move here because he says he's got to be close to his mother, and she lives in Duncan, and that is four miles from Shelby. There are no other houses near us now. Only a few people live out here, Mother says. We leave the town where I grew up with other people next door on both sides of our house, in front, behind, and just a whole town of people. Here, there is no one for miles. Hardface sells corn whiskey in Duncan and Shelby. First, he gets the whiskey in gallon-size bottles from some other place, brings it to our new house, and puts dried peaches or apples in it. He says this makes it taste better. Then he pours it into quart size bottles and sells it. There is a big tree in our backyard, and I like being near it. One day, Mother comes around the house and finds me near the tree. She says, "Hardface is a Christian and you need to be *saved* so he does not get mad. Pray to Jesus to give you a sign so you can be saved."

I say, "Yes, ma'am," and I look up in the sky and start praying to Jesus to give me a sign. Soon I see something move in the sky and run to tell Mother that Jesus gave me a sign. She smiles and tells me that we'll be going to church Sunday, and I will have to give my testimony. Sunday arrives and we go to a small white church about two miles from our house. When we walk inside the church, I see only a few people scattered about and someone sitting in the pulpit. Mother goes to the preacher behind the altar and whispers something to him, and smiling, he gets up and tells everyone that they will have a testimony. They all come to the front of the church and Mother tells me to go up to the front and give my testimony. "Tell them you've been saved," she demands, "and tell them about the sign Jesus gave you." I do this. Now they take me behind the church and walk out in a dirty water place, twist me backward into the water three times.

"In the name of the Jesus, the Father, the Holy Spirit," the preacher says. We get in the car and go home.

Mother sends me to the school in Duncan. It is a church, and Ms. Mayes, a lady from Shelby, teaches all the classes. I must walk to school and back home each day. Ms. Mayes tells me to help her with the kindergarten kids while she teaches the others. One day after school, I get home and Mother comes out to the tree and tells me, "We need money and we're going to move to the Duds

Man of the House

Plantation outside of Shelby." It is thirteen miles east of Shelby, off Highway 32. We do not drink Folgers Coffee and talk at night anymore. Once we get to the new house on the Duds Plantation, I walk through the tall dead grass toward the back and see a red pipe sticking out of the ground with a mouth on it. I do not know what this thing is and go on to another house-like building off to the side. There are bales of hay on the second floor, but now, I do not know these bundles of grass are hay. I have not seen these things before. The first floor is dirt, and there are some rusty tools scattered about. I walk slowly back toward the house and see a yellow-and-black dog lying on the ground with lots of little pups nursing her. One pup wobbles toward me and I pick it up, hold it in my arms, and brush its hair before giving it back to its mother.

I lean over to the mother and begin brushing her face and talking to her. I call her Mary, and with her large brown eyes, she looks up at me. Her soft eyes look like they are smiling. She looks relaxed. I pick up another one of her little wobbling pups and tell her that I will not hurt her baby. I had not seen her when I walked around the back of the house, past the pump to the barn. She and her pups were lying in a batch of dead grass that hid them. Coming back to the house from the barn, I almost stumble on my little family-to-be. I have never had a pet before, and now I have eight: Mary and her seven little ones. Mary's coat of hair is mostly tan with shades of black hair above her eyes, and her puppies look like a rainbow. "Whut chu doin' settin' on yo' lazy azz?!" Hardface yells, shocking me. "Git up offen yo' azz 'n *git ur stick 'n kill dem damn dogs*! Us ain't got no food tu feed dem damn dawgs wid! I sed git up offen' yo' dead azz 'n kill dem gauwd-damn dawgs fo' I pic' up ur stick 'n kill yo' stank-'n black azz! *Move, niggar*!" he demands.

Thunder-struck and incredulous, unable to comprehend the demand to kill my dog and her little puppies, I look back up at him and notice that he has found a large piece of a tree branch and is coming after me with it! I start to get up and take the first deadly whack across my shoulders and tumble to the ground near my dog and her puppies. "Git cho nasty azz zup, nig-gur, lak I tol' chu, 'n kill dem damn dogs 'fo I kill yo black azz!" Whop! he strikes me again. I look around through watery eyes until I find a small stick and limp back to Mary, and looking into her big brown eyes, I see that her eyes have become dull and overcast. Hardface whacks me again and again and begins cursing me until I literally kill my dog and each one of her little puppies. Mary and her puppies do not attempt to run away . . . She does not move at all. She keeps looking at me until her big brown eyes close in death, and her little puppies do the same thing. "Git up offen yo' nasty azz 'n go put dem damn dawgs 'n ur hole obber dare 'n dat ditch!" he barks.

I pick up Mary in my arms, put her babies on top of her tummy, and take them to the ditch, dig a hole in the mud, and lay them in it. "Git cho' black azz back obber har!" Hardface yells at me. "Run! You Black Sap-sucker! Run wen I calls yo' nasty azz!" Crying, I begin running back toward him. A big wood-rat darts across the yard as I am getting near the house, and then he yells, "Kill dat rat 'n skin hit!" I hit the rat with the stick I had used to kill Mary and her little ones. The rat flipped over and wiggled, then it, too, died. "Skin hit 'n git de guts aidder hit, 'n cook dat thang wid sum rice 'n biscuits 'n eat hit!" he demands. Mother stands in the back door with her hands on her hips, watching but not saying anything. I look at her, and she turns back inside of the house and says nothing. I cook the cleaned rat, rice, and gravy, as he demands, and sit down to eat it. I gag and throw up on the floor. "Git cho nasty azz down dare n eat dat shit!" he yells, *"We ain't got no food tur throw-way!"* He is holding a stick and staring through my skin. I eat the gagged rat and rice, and all of the other leavings in the plate.

Outside again, I want to barf, and it will not come out. I go past the pump and sit in the barn for a while. I walk around for a long time and go to the front of the house and see red-and-white cows standing near a barbed wire fence. In kindergarten, I read about the cow that jumped over the moon, and now I see real cows. I cross the gravel road and go up to the fence to look at them. Just then a real big one snorts its nose and runs toward the fence. I turn and run back across the road, and looking back, I see it staring at me. Later I ask Mother about that one and she says that it is a bull. "Stay away from that fence!" A big yellow bus comes by now and Mother says that it is a school bus and takes children to school in Shelby. Time passes before Mother lets me take the bus to Broad Street School. Mother has her first baby girl now, and I have to take care of two babies, and one little brother has started walking. This house has four rooms. Mother and Hardface sleep in the front bedroom, and all of the kids sleep in the second bedroom. The front room has a fireplace, and most of the time when we are all home, we gather in this room. Just behind it is the kitchen. It is easy to hear Mother and Hardface making noise at night.

One day, Mother tells me that she and Hardface are going to the cottonfield and that I will have to stay home and take care of my siblings. Before they leave for the cottonfield, she gives me a long list of tasks to assign to each of my siblings who are old enough to do them and tells me to make sure that they do each task correctly, and if not to "whip their behinds. If I come back home tonight and these things are not done the way I'm telling you, I am going to *beat your butt till you turn as white as rice*!" I talk to each of my siblings who has an assignment and tell them how to do their work. Cluck, my third sibling, says, "Ain't doing 'nuttin!" and I whip him. When Mother and Hardface return home, Cluck runs to Hardface and cries, "Daddy, *he beat me for nuttin*!"

Frantically Hardface unbuckles his belt and begins beating me with the buckle end of the belt! One of the lashes comes across my head and the buckle strikes me in my right eye. The eye bulges out and turns purple. It swells to the size of a golf ball, and Mother screams, "*Honey! Look at his eye*! I think you knocked his eye out! We better get him to the doctor! *Lord, Jesus*!"

They take me to Clarksdale to find an eye specialist to treat my right eye. It is dark now, but one optometrist still has his lights on and urges us to come inside his office. He looks at me and yells, "*What in God's name happened to this child's eye?!*"

Mother drops her head, and Hardface lies, "Doc-dur, dem chullen dey wuz ait-side in de yard fighten' 'n one-uppen pick up ur stick n hit de udden 'n de ai' wid ur stick! Sho' did, Doc-dur!" Mother says nothing, and the doctor rushes me back into his office and, after treating my eye to reduce the inflammation, prescribes glasses for me. Before leaving, the doctor covers my right eye with gauze and tells Mother to bring me back for glasses. Back home, the old habits take over our lives.

Mother has told me how to use the pump in the backyard to get water for cleaning dishes, washing clothes and baby diapers. I must pump it until the water starts coming out of the ground and keep pumping until the bucket on the ground beneath its spout is full, and then haul the gallon bucket of water to the house. Sometimes my hernia bulges out and hurts from hauling the water. I wake early one morning and start for the back door to get out of the house and hide some place. Mother calls and tells me to start making coffee and cooking breakfast for everybody. A while later, she comes into the kitchen and says, "I could smell that coffee. It smells good. Make two cups for me and Hardface." I make the coffee. A few minutes later, Mother and Hardface come into the kitchen, sit at the table, and begin eating breakfast. I peek through a door hole to watch them because I have never seen anyone gobble down biscuits like that before. Once they are finished, I wake up the other kids, clean and clothe them, and bring them into the kitchen and feed them.

Mother calls everyone into the front room and tells us to sit on the floor because "Hardface's got something to tell us!" Mother is smiling and looking at Hardface as he bolts upright in his chair, clears his throat, then says, "Honey," he starts, "Um ma' tell yu' sum-thang dat dun happen las' niate. Whist we sleepin' de Lawd don' kum tu me in ur dream 'n sade, 'Git up 'n go preach de werd!' *Um knot lyin'*. Gawd kum tur me 'n ur dream! He-urs settin' on ur cloud 'n ur cher 'n sade, 'Git up 'n go preach de werd!' 'n I sade, 'Yeas, Lawd! Um ma go 'n preech de Werd, Lawd! I sho' is!'" He stands up, shoves his dirty hands down into his overall's pockets, as his once normally ashen black face lights up. He rolls himself a cigarette, strikes a match and lights it, takes a deep draw on it, and blows the wad of smoke out.

Mother is still looking up at him and she says, "Honey, you're a preacher now! The Lord has called you to preach!"

He starts prancing and suddenly stops, stands still as he looks at Mother and says, "I sho' is, ain't Ur? I sho' Gawd is! De Lawd dunt called me tur preach! I sho' is! Um is Reb-bon Bonner-do! Gut Gawd ur-migh-dy! Whur de Bibber at?!" He and Mother stare at each other until she says, "We'll have to go to the store and get a Bible, honey!" He stares straight through her with his mouth hung open . . . Slowly he turns toward the kitchen and walks out of the back door and disappeared into emptiness. I walk to the barn and hide on the second floor in the sticky hay and lay my head against the wall.

A brown snake moves slowly out of the nearby corner, and I watch its long body disappear through a hole. I cannot see where the snake has gone and rush over and look down into the hole in search of it. The hole seems empty; I can see the bottom floor but nothing else. I walk down to the bottom floor and on out back of the barn and sit on the ground. It is wet, and I back myself onto the wooden part of the barn door's opening. There are lots of trees in the distance, but just ahead of me is a large cornfield with dead stalks leaning toward the ground. A little snail moves silently near my left foot. I lie against the door-facing as the sun begins coming up from behind the distant trees.

I go back to the house and sit on the front porch. Hardface returns after making his rounds to each of the houses in our new cluster of sharecropper families. He returns with an even brighter glow on his face, and Mother urges him to take her to the store to get a Bible since he is now a preacher. "Yea!" he starts, "De fokes obber dare sides de Big Boss Main's house dun ar-reddy ax-ed me tu preech dis Sun-dy hat Miant Oli-ber Baptist Cherch! De sa' dat dey needin' ur preech-chur 'caus'n dey pastur gon' aid-der tawn fur ur-while. I ses sho' I be bliged tu do de Lawd's werk dis Sun-ny, Yar, sur!"

Mother looks at him and says, "You are going to preach this Sunday at the Old Mt. Oliver M.B. Church and we do not even have a Bible in the house?! Let's go to town, honey! We've got to get a Bible for you to start getting ready for your first big sermon, and today is Wednesday. Lord Jesus, honey!" They dash out of the door and jump into his green 1949 Pontiac and drive away without a word to the kids.

Once back home, Mother clears the kitchen table and makes coffee for him so that he can study the Bible and begin practicing his sermon for Sunday. Hardface sits at the end of the table, looking at the big black book in front of him and glancing up at Mother without saying anything. "Do you need something, honey?" she asks nervously. He has not opened the Bible.

"Hell, 'oman, yu' knows Ah kan't reed no buk!" Mother's mouth opens but she does not say anything. Hardface had committed himself to preach a sermon at the area's largest church and could not read.

She turns to me and says, "Put the children to bed!" I put everyone to bed and go in the front room and hear Mother saying, "Honey, let me help you to read a verse and you can take your sermon from that verse."

He says, "Dey wonts me tur preech fum Thurd John sick-teenth."

Mother opens the Bible to the chapter and verse they want him to preach from and begins reading, "And John said . . ." She looks up and he is looking at her. "Come on, honey," she pleads, "repeat after me and soon you're going to know it by heart! Come on, now. And John said . . ."

Man of the House

He looks through her and says, "'N Jonn sade." She continues reading the one verse, but he cannot say anything except "'N Jonn sade . . ," and he stops, looks at her, and says it again. Mother asks him, "What's wrong, honey?"

He retorts,"'Ain't ur gawddamned thang wrong! Hi kum I got-tur har you keep ax-ing me dat fukkin qus-ion?" He stares at her.

"Why don't we go to bed," she starts, "and we can practice some more tomorrow."

He says, "Yea, um don' had hit fur tur-day. Um gwine lay dain 'n sleep fur ur-while."

The morning sunlight lightens the bedroom through the side window, and slowly I wake and go outside and sit in the spot where I held Mary's little pups. Soon I hear Mother calling me to "get in the house and make coffee and breakfast." Hardface gobbles down coffee, biscuits, and syrup, takes a match and lights his rolled cigarette, sucks the food from between his teeth, belches, gets up from the table, and walks out on the front porch. He farts while smoking, and the sound of his gas disposal is heard throughout the house. I am making breakfast for my siblings and myself. Mother goes out on the porch with Hardface. I wake the babies, clean and dress them, and we eat breakfast before I wake the baby and give her a bottle of milk. Mother and Hardface's voices are getting louder as she struggles to get him to read the Bible so he'll be ready to preach Sunday. They practice reading the same scripture over and over and over again, and again and again and forever, and Hardface is not being able to get past "'N jonn sade . . ." Mother begins to look drained and frustrated. The next two days she keeps reading this verse and asking him to repeat after her. It is late Saturday night when he bellows, "Owman, *Ar kan't 'member dat shit!*" He curses a string of words that are barely intelligible.

Early Sunday morning is here, and after breakfast we begin getting ready to go to church. Mother looks worried but says nothing. Once we are ready for church, we all march out of the house and get in the car, and it will not start. Hardface sweats as he uses his foot to turn the thing that turns the engine to make it start. It misfires as he gets dirt on himself. Mother tells him that we'd better start walking. The long winding gravel road is dusty, and by the time we reach the Old Mt. Oliver M.B. Church, each of us needs a bath or at least to clean the dust from our faces. We walk inside and see that the church

Man of the House

is nearly full, and others from throughout the countryside are still arriving and coming in through the doors. The assistant pastor sits in the pulpit and quickly rushes over to meet the new preacher and welcomes him to the seat normally occupied by the pastor. Mother guides us to the front row seat. She now has six boys and girl and is pregnant. We take up most of the front-row seat on the left side of the church, and Hardface is peaking at Mother from around the podium. Beads of sweat run down his face and he has already started wiping away sweat from his face with his handkerchief. The assistant pastor stands up and walks to the altar, clears his throat, and begins his introductory remarks and opening of the services. "Brudders 'n susters, Amain, we is blessed tu be har tu-day! Thank de Lawd! Thank de Lawd!"

The congregation responds with, "Yes, Lawd! Bless de Lawd! Speak Brudder Preacher! Lawd ur mercy!"

He continues, "Us's pastur kan't be har tur-day, Bless de Lawd!" The congregation's feet begin tapping the floor, and hands are clapping, bodies rotating in rhythm with the chant, and the congregation begins singing "Amazing Grace"—Mother's favorite song, to which she sings too. The congregation is now on its feet, clapping hands and singing with body and soul. The wooden church seems to be rocking with an invisible force. One large lady shout and flings her arms about. I look around and see a little girl rushing away to her mother's lap. One man rushes over to help the shouting lady, and another lady begins fanning her. The assistant pastor sways as he speaks in front of the podium, "Amazing Grace," he says, "God's Amazing Grace!"

"Brudders 'n susters," he preaches, "We gon ni inner-duce de Reb-ben Hardface! De Lawd jes called him tur preech de Werd, 'n he gon preach tur us tur-day whist us's Pastur aidder town. De Lawd knows when we needs him, 'n He don sunt de Reb-ben Hardface to give us de Werd tu-day! Lemme inner-duce de Reb-ben Hardface! Reb-ben Hardface!" he says, bowing to Hardface and backing away to take his seat. Hardface stands, and moving up to the podium, says, "'N Jonn sade. 'N Jonn sade . . ." He stares at Mother, and she drops her head in silence. "'N Jonn sade . . ." he continues, still looking at Mother.

The assistant pastor rushes up to the altar and says, "That's wonderful, Brudder Preacher," and taking over the podium, he begins quickly closing out the service, and we are back on the gravel road home.

Man of the House

Silence surrounds us on the way back home. We walk slowly, and just as we are crossing the gravel road intersection near the large ammonia tank, a small red tractor pulls up and stops close to us. The man on the tractor is Dave. He shuts off the engine and jumps down to the ground, rushes over to Hardface and, without a word, punches Hardface's face, knocking him backward. Dave gets back on his tractor and drives away! Hardface, struggling to get his balance in the presence of Mother and all of the kids, puffs up his shoulders and, looking at Mother, says, "Honey, whut chu thank I odder do? You thank I odder kill dat Mudder-fukk'ing niggar! Whut he hit me fur?! You thank I odder go home 'n git my shotgun 'n kill dat Mudder-fukker?" Mother's face is a smirk as she looks at him and begins walking on toward the house. Once home, Mother goes inside, lies on the bed, and falls asleep. Hardface goes to the back porch and begins mixing dried peaches in a gallon-size bottle of corn whiskey.

The whiskey changes color, and he begins pouring it into quart-size Mason jars for sale. With a few quart-size bottles in hand, he takes off for the other houses to sell it. And even though he cannot count numbers, he knows that one quarter equaled " two bits," two quarters equaled four bits, three quarters equaled six bits, and four quarters equaled a dollar. Someone had taught him that. Hardface sticks to his new title while avoiding the church.

Ron Sams is the foreman on the plantation and lives with his family in the big white house in the center of this village. Several sharecropper houses and a large barn are close by the big house, and a very large white ammonia tank sits out from it and about a city block away from us. The leaking sounds of the ammonia tank can be heard by everyone on the plantation, and the wind moves the leaking ammonia about the plantation. Its smell is strong. One cottonfield stretches from the gravel road at the intersection where Dave punched Hardface to the deep curve in the road near our house and back to the forest. Our family works mostly on this cottonfield, and Mother has a large vegetable garden behind the house. We begin chopping cotton in late March and picking cotton late August. All the while, the ammonia tank leaks, and the wind blows it. During cotton-chopping season, from March to late July, we go to the cottonfield and chop the weeds from around the cotton. Occasionally a spray-aircraft descends from the sky, without notice, and sprays DDT over the growing cotton to kill boll weavers, and we are soaked by the spray.

Man of the House

I hear the Big Bend clock rattling its loud clicking noise in the other room where Mother and Hardface sleep. It stops, and I get out of bed to make coffee and breakfast for them. Darkness is everywhere, and I tiptoe over my siblings who are sleeping on blankets on the floor. Almost all of us got in the bed. Every night we scramble to get a spot on the bed. Somebody will not make it or squeezes in some space to sleep. We pile out of the house before the sun rises with hoes and get to the beginning of the cottonfield near the ammonia tank and smell its seeping gas. There is almost no wind blowing now, and we can see a little distance down the cottonfield the Big House and shadows of the other sharecropper houses on the other side of the road going around the plantation and barns. "File dem hoes!" Hardface yells, looking at me. Mother has a smirk on her face, and she is looking at me too. I get the file. It has a dried piece of corncob on the handle for gripping. If the file slips and the hoe touch my skin, it slices my skin, and I have to be really careful. I put the hoe blade on my left knee and file it to make the blade sharp for chopping cotton. First, I file the outside of the hoe-blade four or five times, then turn the hoe straight up and file the inside of the blade the same number of strokes. "Hurr-rup, niggar! You ain't got all fuckin' day tur file dem hoes!" Hardface yells.

    I speed up a little with the next hoe and the next one, till they are all filed. Mother tells each of the kids which row of cotton to chop and we begin work. The baby is home, and I'll have to run back and change her diaper and feed her in a little while. Mother gives me the lunch bag to take to the shade trees at the other end of the cottonfield and says, "Hurry back. We've got to start work in a few minutes." I run to the other end of the cottonfield with our lunch and get back to start chopping cotton with the others. Occasionally, I look down the long cottonfield and get a feeling for how long it takes us to get from one end of the cottonfield to the other. After a few times of doing this, I know about when we will get a rest break and eat lunch. After lunch, I do the same thing, and soon I know how many rows we chop before I get a chance to go back home. We get to the end of the cottonfield and begin chopping the next set of cotton rows headed back to the beginning of the field. It is hot now and almost time for lunch. A twister springs up near the beginning of the field, spinning and getting bigger as it spins and blows up dirt into the air. We keep chopping cotton and keep glancing at the twister. My hoe is getting dull, and

I am slipping behind. I chop faster and catch up to ward off a beating. "Move, niggar!" Hardface yells at me. My siblings chop faster too. The twister spins and grows, moving toward us, then it stays in one spot and spins faster and faster, making dirt foam into the air, and just before it begins crossing us, Mother yells, "Cover your faces with your shirts!" We stop and cover our faces till the twister passes. "What time is it?" she asks, looking up in the sky.

Hardface barks, "Hit 'out time tur eat! De sun at high noon, ni." We drop our hoes and walk back toward the shade trees, sit down, and wait for Mother to take out the Campbell's soup cans and give them to me to pull off their tops. She pours out about half of each can on each plate. Hardface gets served first, and he eats a whole canful, tells the kid closest to the gallon-size sweetened water bottle to "gimme sum ur dat worter obber dare!" He gulps down the water, belches, sucks the food from between his teeth, rolls a cigarette, lights it, and leans back against the tree while smoking.

Mother finishes her food, drinks a small cup of sweet-water, and lies back on the ground and sleeps for a few minutes. When she wakes, we go back to our hoes and begin work again. She sleeps only a few minutes each time she takes a nap. We get back to work, and I can see other sharecropper families in the distance working in another field. No one talks while chopping cotton, and the sun is cooking our skin now. The air is almost still, and sweat rolls down my back. I cannot stop and keep working, like the others, struggling to keep up with Mother and Hardface. One of my siblings gets behind, and Mother rushes over to help him catch up and then gets back to her row. About mid-afternoon, the sky begins to darken, and the wind stirs the trees a little. Blackbirds are flying and lighting on the electrical wires running to the different houses. Cows are walking slowly toward the trees, and Mother says, "It's going to storm soon." The clouds darken and the wind grows stronger and stronger. Almost every afternoon, it storms. I am praying to God to make a flood like he did when Noah was building his boat.

Thunder rumbles lightly, and Mother says, "We need to get ready to go home before it storms."

Hardface looks at her and says, "Yeah, you right." It is too late. Lightning flashes in long, jagged strikes, making a loud noise, ripping the skies. Thunder rumbles louder, and large drops of rain fall in spats, growing slowly into a storm as the clouds grow ever darker. "We bet-ur git tur de hase," he says to Mother, as they lead the way, rushing toward the house. Lightning and thunder are getting stronger and happening more often as the clouds turn almost grey black. Mother begins running, then stopping and holding her tummy, taking a deep breath, and then running again. Hardface is making it fast toward the house and not looking back. I take Mother's hoe and ask if she needs help. She holds on to my left shoulder while rushing to the house. It is storming now as we get to the house, wet, and I take the hoes and put them underneath the tree. They all go inside of the house, and I walk out to the barn and sit inside on the first-floor ground. It is quiet in here and I see bugs and rats, spiderwebs, and old, rusted farm machine pieces against the other wall lying about. Thunder, lightning, and rain. The storm roars and water begin running down the garden and cotton rows. Wind blows rain through the big open barn doors on each side and the air is cool. A long black snake comes in out of the rain and moves along the wall. It stops and slowly draws itself into an S-shape, lunges, and catches a mouse in its mouth.

Days and nights pass. The cotton grows taller, and stalks become bushes during the cotton-chopping season. We are chopping one day, and the cotton is almost waist high when a spray airplane turns above the trees ahead of us and, slowly moving down close to the cotton, begins gushing out a cloud of DDT as it moves fast, straight toward us. "*Cover your faces!*" Mother yells. It moves fast toward the end of the cottonfield and goes back up in the air, makes a wide turn, and comes back down from behind us, gushing out a cloud of DDT. Bolls of cotton are growing on the bushes now, and the spray plane sneaks up on us while we are working lots of times. We get back to work as soon as the spray plane moves across the field away from us and then on to the other cottonfields. We return to school now and study till it is time to pick cotton in August. Time in school flies by, and I barely get to know my teachers and the other students before it is time to pick cotton again. Soon the big yellow school bus stops coming to our house, and we are back in the cottonfield.

Dave brings a big empty cotton trailer and parks it at the beginning of the cottonfield near our house, unhooks the trailer from the tractor, and leaves. It is

Man of the House

early in the morning when we get to the cottonfield and get our new cotton sacks. The cotton trailer is up above my head, and I must figure out a way to get my cotton sack up to the top of it and then get it over into the trailer to empty it without making my hernia bulge out and hurt. It is almost light enough to see the cotton bolls now, and we move close to the cotton. Mother tells me which two rows I must pick and says, "I want two hundred pounds of cotton out of you today!" It has rained during the night, and the cotton leaves are wet, the ground is soggy, and there is water in patches along the cotton rows.

"Git tur werk!" Hardface yells, "Hit day-time, na!" It is barely daylight, and we begin picking the wet cotton from the top of the bush, working our way through it to the bottom, twisting across to the row on our left side without looking up, and begin picking the cotton on the first bush from the bottom up, back to the right-side row from the top down, and again to the bottom of the last row bush and back to the top of the bush on that side. Dew has soaked the fluffy cotton inside the bolls and the cotton seems to almost hang out of the bolls. I must pick a lot now before the dew dries by the morning sun, because the wet cotton weighs more than when it is dry and that helps me to get the two hundred pounds Mother tells me to pick. In the late afternoon, I have to work faster if I feel like I might not get the two hundred pounds; and if I am scared really bad, I throw lots of dirt in the cotton sack to make it weigh more. We pick the cotton in this way until the cotton sack gets stuffed near the opening at our shoulders. Mother and Hardface are wearing kneepads and pick cotton from the bottom up most of the time. Kids do not get knee pads until they grow up.

My sack is getting heavy with the cotton near the mouth of the sack, and I get on my back and use my feet to stuff it down to the bottom of the sack, then get back up, put the strap over my head, and get back to picking cotton again. I notice Hardface getting a handful of mud and throwing it in his sack. Mother smiles at him, and he grins. The cotton in the sack soaks up the water in the patches of the rows while I am moving along and picking cotton. The cotton sack becomes heavier and heavier and more difficult to pull through the muddy space between the two cotton rows. Hardface sees Jim walking out toward us, and I see him jerking a cotton stalk out of the ground and running over toward me. "Nig-gar! *You see dat White main coming*! Git tur pickin' cutton *fass-er*! *Move, nig-gar*!" he says, whacking me across the back and head with the root-end of the cotton stalk. He rushes back to his own cotton sack and burrows himself down between the bushes, picking faster and faster and still faster. Mother is working faster and faster too, and all of us kids are struggling to keep up with them.

Ron walks slowly over to Hardface and says, "Hardface!" and before Ron can say more, Hardface comes up out of the cotton bushes, looking down toward the ground, saying, "Ya-sur!"

Ron suddenly reaches the sides of his waist with each hand and jerks his pants up while saying to Hardface, "I want you to weigh the cotton and give me a tally at the end of the day."

Hardface rushes to say, "Ya-sur, I show will, sur, I show will," grinning and nodding his head up and down.

"I'll send Dave over to get the tally," he says, leaving.

"Ah show will, sur. Ah show will!" Ron has now gone away, walking back toward the Big House. Hardface stares at Mother while she continues picking cotton. My cotton sack is stuffed near the mouth of the sack again, and my hernia has bulged out. I am in lots of pain and tell Mother that my hernia is hurting. "Lay down on the sack for a while and let it go down. When it stops hurting, get back to work!" I get the cotton strap off my shoulders and lie down on the sack underneath the cotton bushes.

"Dat white main gong git mad if'n he see dat niggar hidin' unner dem cotton stalks lak dat, honey," Hardface complains. She does not say anything, and Hardface gets back to work. Soon she tells Hardface that he needs to take her cotton sack to the scales and weigh it. He lifts the sack onto his right shoulder and walks back to the trailer.

They return and I hear Hardface telling Mother, "Dat niggar still layin' on his ass unner dem stalks!"

Mother comes over to me and asks, "How are you feeling?" I tell her that I am still hurting, and she says, "Just lay there till you stop hurting."

She goes back, and I hear Hardface saying, "Dat niggar ain't wuffer shit!" When I stop hurting, I get back to work, and soon my cotton sack is full, and I tell Mother that I need to get it weighed.

"Honey," she calls to Hardface, "You need to weigh his cotton."

Man of the House

I watch him stare at her and yell, "You know I kan't count dem nummers!" I lift the cotton sack onto my right shoulder and start walking toward the trailer. My hernia bulges out again in pain. I am afraid to stop because I might get a beating again. I make it to the trailer and hook the sack onto the scale. Mother tells Hardface how much my cotton sack weighs, and he says, "Sho is, Honey! Dat's de 'mount. We has tu put a tally lak de White main sa-s." She does not have anything to write with or write on and tells him that she'll keep the amount in her head till she gets a pencil and some paper. He yells at me, "Thow dat sack up in de trailer and empty hit!" I pull the top of the sack off the scale and try holding it while climbing into the trailer, then pulling it to get it up to the top and over in the trailer.

Mother says, "Hardface, you're going to have to help him."

He stares through me and yanks the sack off the scale, shoves it up over the top of the trailer, and yells at me, "Empty hit, *Sucker*, 'n git cho stanking ass back tur werk!" He and Mother go on back to the cottonfield, and when I am finished emptying the cotton sack, I am in lots of pain and slowly get out of the big trailer and walk back to the cotton field and lie down on my empty sack.

Mother comes over and asks, "Are you hurting?" I say yes, and she frowns. "Lay down there for a while and I'll come back and check on you. We need the money. Lord knows we need the money!" she says, leaving. Day after day, we work in the cottonfield, and during each day, I pick cotton with the others when my hernia is not hurting too much to drag the cotton sack.

One afternoon while home, Hardface gets angry with Mother. He grabs a handful of her hair, jerks her head back, and pulls a switchblade knife around her throat, yelling, "'owman, don't be fuckin' wid me! *Ail cut cho goaddammed hed off!*" She is about eight months pregnant with his second daughter now. Mother becomes an angel and talks him into taking the knife away from her throat, promising him the best meal he's ever eaten and a wonderful night in bed. Meanwhile, I am sitting near the fireplace and slowly get the fireiron and scoot back behind them. He lets Mother go, and she moves about while he stands flexing his muscles and boasting that he could have killed her if he had wanted to do it. I am behind him now and, standing up, I aim the fireiron, and leaning back gives my whole body strength to slice his head in half, and as I move to strike him, Mother grabs the other end of the iron and jerks it out of my hand. Quickly she writes a note and asks Hardface to go to the store and buy the food she wants to cook him a delicious meal. Smiling, while flipping his switchblade knife back into his right pocket, he rushes out of the house and drives away to the store with her note.

Chapter 6
A New Day

*Be grateful for whoever comes,
because each has been sent as
a guide from beyond.*
— Rumi

She has given birth to one daughter and one son for him and is pregnant with his second daughter now. Mother tells me to go tell the foreman that Hardface threatened to kill her and ask him to take us away to a safe place. I run across the cottonfield to the Big House back door, knock, and when the door opens, I see Ron and his wife, Sandy, standing there talking. I tell them what Mother said, and see their faces become stern, as she says, "*Go!*" and he looks at me and says, "*Git in the truck! I'll be right there!*" and looking at his wife, he says, "I'll be back soon, honey!" Just as I get in the truck, Ron jerks open the driver's side of the pickup truck and starts the engine. He jerks it into gear and backs the truck, turning and speeding out of his yard and on to our house. He drives into our yard, jumps out, and helps Mother get into the front seat, and then comes back and helps me round up all of the other kids, beddings and clothes, food, and everything else we can find in the house, and stuff it all in the back of the pickup truck. Everybody and everything possible have been loaded into the back of the pickup truck, and some of the younger kids are piled into the cab with Mother and Ron.

Man of the House

He drives away to his farm in Cascilla in the quiet night. We are safe now. Mother is eight months pregnant and cannot work. We do not have a bed for Mother to sleep on when we get to the new house in Cascilla, not much food, and no water to bath in or drink. When we get to his house in Cascilla, Ron helps me to get Mother inside our new house with the babies and unloads the truck. Once everyone and everything is inside of the house, I ask Ron for a job. He promises to come back the next day and talk to me about it, tells me not to worry, and he leaves. It is dark inside the house, and I find the kerosene lamp and light it, lay blankets on the floor for Mother and the babies. Mother is five feet two inches tall, very plump, and it is difficult for her to get down all the way to the floor to lie down. I help her, and when she is relaxed, I get the babies and put them beside her, lay blankets on the floor in the kitchen for everyone else, and lock the front door before going to bed.

As usual we have our morning oatmeal, and Mother and I drink Folger's Coffee for breakfast while the other kids run out to discover our new surroundings and play. And, as promised, Ron arrives about noon and gives me a job plowing one of his cottonfields with a mule at $1.50 per day, six days a week, from sunrise till dark. Ron tells me about the school bus that takes kids to different schools in Charleston, and as my siblings get ready for school, I get ready for work so we can have food and clothes. Ron gives me a ride in his truck to the Big House, and while walking around his barn where the tractor and tools are, he shows me the mule in the pasture just ahead. We go out and get the mule, and he shows me how to hook up the bridle and plowing gear, plow, and shows me how to get the mule to pull the plow when I tip the point of it into the ground and plow the cottonfield. He asks me to follow him to the cottonfield the first day so I will know how to get there with the mule. I walk along as he drives the mule with the plow hooked up to it, going across the pasture and past the mule shed, on into the woods and out to the cottonfield.

He shows me how to get the mule and plow lined up to turn over the soil and then disconnects the mule from the plow to leave it in the field. Now I can just hook up the mule and drive him out to the cottonfield without having to struggle with the plow on the way. I am fourteen now, and before Ron leaves, he tells me about the other two families on his farm, then says, "Old Hank jes kinda stays home. He drinks …" We walk over to the small, fenced pen and he shows me the little pet deer he has. "Got her when she was a baby," he says. She comes to the fence, and I touch her soft wet nose. Soon Ron moves his family back home from Shelby to Cascilla, and I see him sometimes when going or coming from the cottonfields. He uses the tractor to plow the other field for a while, then shows me how to drive it and put the mule away back in his stall. Every Saturday after work, he pays me ten dollars for the week, and Mother takes it all when I get home.

One Sunday, Will, Zarv, and I go across the road to cut down a tree to make firewood and we see a black-and-white animal. It starts to run away, and we run after it. Zarv gets a head start and is ahead of us. Will yells, "It's a mink! We can make some money!" The animal stops and raises its rear end and pees. The air is filled with a bad, bad smell, and we run for the woods. The smell stays with us, and it is really strong.

We cannot get away from the smell and go back home to take a bath. Mother turns up her nose and asks, "What is that *smell?!* *Jesus*!" We rush, together, to tell her that a black-and-white animal did it. "A skunk!" she screams. "Go take a *bath*!" We bathe with lye soap, and the smell stays the same. Monday morning my siblings go to school if they are old enough, and I go to work. I must stay out of school this year to buy food and other things we need. I stop to touch the deer and talk to her one day, and Ron comes out. He talks to me about the deer and gives me thirteen pigeons with different colors that he has in an aviary and says that I can take them home when I build my own aviary.

On the first day of plowing in this red clay, I raise the plow handles to make the blade go into the hard ground and hit the mule with the leather straps to make it pull the plow and start turning over the red clay rock-like soil. Once we get to the end of the cottonfield, the mule screeches, rises up into the air on its front legs, and begins hopping backward onto the plow! Its hind feet straddle the plow, and I pull the reigns to stop the mule. It twists itself to the left and jerks the plow around, snorting, and darting from the right to the left side before stumbling backwards and throwing its front feet off to the left and pulling the plow and me around back toward the beginning of the cottonfield. I stop the mule and go back and see what the problem is. At the spot where the mule had raised himself off its front feet and into the air and stumbled backward over onto the plow, there is a drop-off into a really deep ravine, and the mule had gotten to the edge of it. The cliff edge drops down into the bottom of the deep ravine.

I stand at the edge of the ravine and look down into the bottom. It is wide and deep, with lots of shapes. The colors are greyish-white and red. It goes on and on, with trees on the top of it. I want to stay here and look—just stay here. It is quiet and nice. I want to go down to the bottom and walk down there. It is silent here. The trees are pretty, and the ravine is pretty. The mule snorts and I get back to work, remembering the unruly shapes and the indefinite length to the bottom. It is a vast opening and deeper than anything I have ever seen. I am alone with the mule and no one to talk to about the ravine! I like the magic and beauty of it. It is silent and dry at the bottom. At the end of the day, Ron comes out to the mule barn to talk to me. "You know how to drive that galddamned tractor thar?"

I shake my head and say, "No, sir."

He gets onto it and says, "Kum-meer, I'm going to show you how to drive this damn tractor. That mule's too slow." I watch while he turns the key to start the tractor. "Hold the clutch down with the left foot, and this here over here is the break! Push it down with your right foot when you gotta stop her! Now just hook that disc to it tomorrow morning and start cuttin' up that cottonfield. That mule's too damn slow. I'll be back in 'er kuppla days. Here's ten dollars to buy y'all sum food!"

I get onto the tractor and look at the different parts of it. The big steering wheel in front and in front of my face has lots of little meters. I have never driven a motorized vehicle before. I turn the key and the motor starts running. *Damn*! Just like that! I turn the big red tractor's engine off and walk home. I never drove Hardface's car; and he had to stick a crankshaft in the front of it and had to turn if really hard to make the engine start. This tractor starts with a key switch. When I get back home and tell Mother that I got paid, she yells, "Give it here!" and *takes all my money*. She talks about all the things she is going to buy when we go shopping. When I begin telling her about the tractor, she is making a list of things she will buy with my money. She does not hear me. The next morning, I head to work and hook the tractor and disc without a problem. The mule blows his nose while I am driving past him, looks at me with his left eye, turns his head away, and blows his nose again. I put the tractor in second gear with the disc raised and go on to the cottonfield and start plowing the ground. My legs are short, and I have to sit on the edge of the seat to reach the clutch and brake. On the edge of the seat, I shove the clutch in, shift the gears into first when turning at the ends of the cottonfield, and then back into second to plow the ground.

I soon become relaxed driving the tractor. There is one other cottonfield to plow after this one and I go there when I finish here. Then I come back here to the first field and cut the cotton rows, fertilize the ground, plant the seeds, and go back and do the same thing in the other field. Within a few weeks, Mother and a couple of my siblings and I begin chopping cotton. It is that time of year for using a hoe to chop through the lined rows of cotton growing out of the ground and create space between one or two seedlings the width of the hoe's blade, and then go to the next couple of seedlings and chop just past those and create another hoe-space, and on and on down the cotton row to the end and begin another row to do the same. We work this way until we clean away all the grass from around the cotton seedlings and create space so that each seedling will have space to grow to become a full cotton stalk and not be choked down by grass, weeds, and vines. We wear long-sleeved shirts and long pants to keep the bugs and mosquitos from biting us.

It gets really hot when the sun is in the center of the sky, and that is when we can go to the end of the cottonfield where the Mulberry trees are and eat sardines, polk 'n' beans, and mulberries. We work in the open sun with not a shade tree in sight except for the forest at the beginning of the cottonfield. When the sun seems to be in the center of the sky, we assume it is about noon, and we stop for a thirty-minute lunch break. We walk to the beginning of the cottonfield where there are trees and sit on the ground underneath a mulberry tree to eat cans of sardines or polk 'n' beans and saltine crackers, drink water, and get back to work. Mother lies on the ground and sleeps for about five minutes after eating lunch, and sometimes she stops in the middle of the cottonfield, stands up straight, and braces herself with the hoe handle under her chin. She cups her hands on top of the hoe handle and rests her chin on top of her hands and sleeps. Then, feeling refreshed, she gets back to work for hours at a time. We chop cotton in a rhythmic manner that keeps all of us alongside each other. We chop around the growing cotton by starting on the opposite side of the cotton row, cutting just beneath the dirt with the hoe to chop away the grass, and then slice through the cotton stalks where we have created the space. We then chop down the inside of the row where we cut beneath the earth's crust to clean away the grass near our feet. While stepping back, we avoid cutting ourselves with the sharp blades. Sometimes Mother stays home with the baby and lets my siblings go to school, especially when she is nursing the baby.

Mother has a bed now, and she sleeps in the front room where the fireplace keeps her and the babies warm. I have a flashlight and help Will, Zarv, and Cluck with their homework before going to bed. On Sundays, I build an aviary for my pigeons, using small trees and wire Ron has given me to cover the sides and the top. When it is ready, Ron gives me the pigeons, and I find empty soda bottles and cans to buy food for them from the general store. I bring the pigeons home and put them in the aviary and watch them. I am listening to the music they sing when they talk to each other. Mother comes up from behind me and says, "Hurry and kill those pigeons so we can have *some meat on the table*!" I tell her that Ron just gave them to me! They are my pets! "*We need meat on the table*! Now *do what I say* and clean them so we can have some meat on the table!" I do it. When I start back to school in November, Mother tells me that I've got to make sure my siblings are quiet on the school bus, and I have to make sure they are all on the bus when we get ready to come back home.

One day when I am talking to the deer, Ron comes over and asks me how the pigeons are doing, and I tell him that Mother made me kill them so she could have meat on the table. He says, "Okay. You can ride the horses when you're not working." He has a breeding pair of horses, and I start riding them. One is tan and one is dark brown. And now that I use the tractor to do lots of things on the farm, I do not have to smell the gas from the mule's stomach when I am working. The feed store sells garden seed packs and lets me sell them to people around in Cascilla. I go to one house and meet a Mrs. Kasey and her daughter, Tee. Mrs. Kasey buys some garden seeds, and I get a penny for each pack she buys. I like Tee, too, and we play for a while before I go. Mrs. Kasey asks about Mother and my siblings, and when I tell her where we live, she says she knows that house and she hopes to meet Mother.

Man of the House

    Sundays are days for chopping down trees and splitting them into blocks for the fireplace and smaller pieces for the kitchen stove. My hernia flares up sometimes, and I stop long enough for it to go back to normal and then get back to work. I get home from school one day and Mother says, "Mr. Hank scares me!" Hank is our alcoholic neighbor who lives between our house and the Big House. There is another house on the hill behind Hank's house too. Mother says that Hank saw her coming down the gravel road and began yelling at her, "Come 'ere, niggra!" She says that she ran for the Big House. Old Hank, as everyone calls him, is a loner and drinks corn whiskey most of the time. We see him drunk, sitting on his front porch in the early morning hours when going to the cottonfields. Sometimes I see him drunk, leaning in his chair and smoking a cigarette, when I go to work, and when he sees me, he'll say something about niggars. Most days he sits in his straw-bottomed chair and sleeps. As Mother and I leave home together the next morning before daylight on her way to work in the Big House, Hank starts out of his front door, wobbling back and forth as he seems to struggle to get into his chair. He sees us and begins yelling, "Heeeeey, yer Galddamned Niggurs!" Mother runs for the Big House, and he talks to me. "Um-ma... Um-ma... kum ait dere 'n cut chere nuts out, boy! Yer ... Galdamned it! Um mur *White Main*! Yer *hear me*?! Um ... I say, um-ma *White* Main, Galddamned hit!" He is wobbling and threatening, and struggling to stand, with the quart bottle of whiskey in his right hand. I watch and listen to Hank. He spills a bit of whiskey out of his Mason jar and curses, "Galddamned it! Look whut chu Mutherfukin' Niggur done made me waste ma ... ma Galddamned whiskey! Al kill yer! Galddamned Nig-ger! Sun-ser-bitch!" He wobbles backward, hugging his bottle close to his chest, staggering back and sits down on his chair. He hangs his head over the bottle and stares down into it.

    I walk on toward the Big House and see Mother standing at the gate. I open the fence-gate and we walk past the deer to the back door of the Big White House and go inside. I go out in the pasture and ride one of the horses before going back home. I ride the horses and learn how to make them raise themselves up into the air and stand on their hind legs. When I ride the horses, I always ride at full speed across the pasture, jumping ditches and cutting sharp corners. One time, I was riding really fast, and the horse saw something that scared her, and she stopped really quick, and I fell off her back.

Man of the House

This spring, the crops are turning into summer cotton stalks with growing buds and there are lots of boll weevils on them. I go with Ron one day to spot check the growing cotton in one field. I see how he pulls back the leaves to check the bolls for boll weavers. He curses when he sees a boll weevil hole in a cotton bud. Silently I pray for them to multiply, because the sooner the cotton is gone, the sooner I get back to school. I feel bad for Jim because he wants the money, and I feel bad for me because I want to go back to school.

One day at the end of the day, I am going home I cross a small creek with cool water running over gravel rocks. I get on my belly and begin drinking from the cool stream. The cool, fresh water tastes good. Something catches my attention from my right eye. I raise myself up slightly and see a large snake. We stare at each other as I scoot backward and out of its reach. The thick snake's colors blend in great with the colors of the rocks and pebbles in the creek. When I see Ron, I ask him about snakes that lie in the creek water, and he says that they are water moccasins and can kill me. The weather is clear next morning, and Mother wants money, so we all go to the cottonfield. It is Saturday and so we work till noon and start back home. We get out of the wooded path that goes to the cottonfield, and at once, we all hear a rattlesnake's tail. Mother and my siblings see it too and run off to the side. Mother screams: *"Kill that snake! It's a rattlesnake!"* The snake lies on the ground underneath a tree with its tail raised and the rattles vibrating like magic. It is pretty and maybe scared of us too. I do not want to hurt it. Mother screams again, *"Kill it!"* I remember seeing a rattlesnake in a book and this one is more beautiful.

I walk slowly till I get close to the snake, raise the hoe, and chop its head off. We walk on home. The clouds are getting dark behind us, and we walk faster to get home before the storm begins. A twister springs up ahead of us, and Mother says "Cover your eyes" to everyone, and holding the baby, she walks faster and faster. This twister is small and does not make much dust coming toward us. It is spinning and looks like an ice cream cone with the tip on the ground. It starts and stops, spinning and spinning, then moves fast going past us. The clouds are getting darker and darker. Large raindrops start to fall, and we rush faster to get home. We get home, rushing through the pasture, and get inside just as the rain begins to pour down. The earth's smell fills the air, and it is getting cooler now. I sit on the front porch and listen to the rain fall on the tin roof. Once the cotton-chopping season is over in August, we stay home and work. I help Mother with the babies and go out to cut firewood for the winter. Sometimes Will helps me cut the trees with a cross-cut saw that I borrowed from Ron. Sometimes we sit on logs and find dead weeds, break them into small pieces, and try to smoke them like the grown folks' smoke cigarettes. The heat burns my tongue and I stop smoking the weed. Will does not like getting burnt either and he stops too.

The sun is rising this morning and I am on my way to work. Just ahead of me I see three White boys walking toward me and looking at me. Something is about to happen. I don't know what and I do not feel right. "Hey, Niggar!" one yells, "Drop yer draws and let us see what cher got!" I am looking at him and see his friends grinning. They are walking across the road towards me now, and I cannot beat all three of them, and I know it. I drop my pants and draws. One says, "*Hell, man,*" looking at the others, "*my* thang's *bigger than his*!"

Another says, "*Mine's bigger than yours!*"

The first snaps back, "*Lies!* Mine's *bigger* than yers!" and each one drops his pants to show whose penis is the largest. I pull my clothes back on and walk off.

The White family living in the bigger house on the hill behind old Hank's house works in the first cottonfield, and we go and pick cotton in the second cottonfield. This family has a little boy with one arm that ends at the elbow. One Sunday morning, the little kid comes to our house and stands in the ditch out front, yelling, "Niggur! Niggur! You gon' come outside 'n play wid me?! Niggur!"

Mother whispers to me, "Go see what he wants!" I walk out through the front door, and immediately I hear the front door's lock click into place. I know that I cannot go back inside until I solve the problem. We look at each other, and he says, "Hey, Niggur, you gon play wid me?"

I walk out to meet him and say, "I do not play with anybody who calls me a bad name."

He looks shocked. "Whut's ur bad name?" he asks.

"Niggur is a bad name," I tell him.

"I didn't *know* that! I *swear tur God*, I didn't *know* that!" he says. "So, what's yo' name?" I tell him, and he promises never to call me a bad name again. He is crying, and we shake hands, and he stops crying. We play for a while shooting marbles that he brought in his pocket. His right arm is full length, and he

Man of the House

shoots marbles with the right hand and tells me that he does not go to school anymore because other kids make fun of him for having a short left arm. On Sundays he comes to visit sometimes, and we play together. Most times, I work in the field, just as his family does.

The sun is getting hot one morning when we're working in the field, and Mother sees old Hank wobbling along the gravel road, headed toward us, yelling, "*Goddamed Niggars!*" and Mother says to me, "Here comes Mr. Hank! Go tell Mr. Sams to make him leave us alone!" I run to the back door of Jim's house and tell him what Mother said. He rushes out of the house and towards Hank, yelling, "*Hank! Git your ass back home!*" Hank lowers his head and turns back toward his house, and I go on back to the cottonfield. Ron goes back home. November comes; most of the cotton has been picked, and we all go to school in Charleston. When we get back home, Mother goes to the Big House to cook dinner for the family, and I check on the babies and get wood for the fireplace. Our dinner is ready, and everyone eats and then goes outside to play in the yard.

At the end of the first school day, we all get back on the bus and ride home. Mother is ready for work and stops me at the door, saying, "Mr. Hank *scared me* yesterday! Come with me to work." We walk along the gravel road on our way to the Big House, and just as we get near old Hank's house, he begins yelling, "*Goaddamned Niggars! Um-ma cut cho nuts off, boy! Ya her me*?! Um-ma *White* main! Um-ma *White main*, you hear me?!" Mother rushes along and I look at poor old Hank, struggling to get out of his chair with the whiskey bottle in his right hand. He looks up from his porch floor where he has spilled a little of the whiskey and yells, "Look-it what chu made me do! *You son-sa-bitching niggar*! Um-ma *cut cher goddamned nuts off!* Do you *know* Um-ur *White* main, niggar?!"

Hank wobbles back to his chair and sits down, and I go on to find Mother standing at the barbed-wire fence, holding her right hand over her heart, saying, "*He scares me!*"

As soon as we get inside the back door, Princess, one of Jim's three daughters, comes running to me, grabs my right hand and says, "Come play with me! *Come onnnnnnnnnn, now!* You *gotta play with me!*" Mother freezes but cannot do anything because even the youngest of Whites is superior to all Blacks, and we both *know* it. We know this Jim Crow truth deep in our guts, our hearts, souls, and everything else! I follow Princess into her bedroom. Her bright eyes are radiant as she begins jumping up and down on the bed. Each time she bounces down, facing me with a bright smile, her legs open and her butt hits the bed. I notice that she is not wearing panties. Suddenly Mother jerks me by my shirt collar and says to Princess, submissively, "Sorry, ma'am," and says to me, "I need you to go out back and get some wood for me real quick! I've got to cook!" I turn to go and see Princess pouting. Once out of the back door, Mother says, "*Go home! NOW!*" She comes home after work, her small brown eyes wracked with fear, and says, "*They're probably gonna want to kill you for looking at that White girl!* And *she was naked, too! Jesus!*" She *scares* me! Days and months pass in our now *silent* house. Nothing happens to me. Day after day and night after night Mother scares me half to death with stories about Black boys and men who have been castrated, beaten, or burned to death for "*just looking at a White girl!*"

I am walking down the hall one day, on my way to my chemistry class. Passing the principal's office, I see from the corner of my left eye a big black board with lots of white papers on it and stop to quickly see what it is. There are white sheets of paper tacked to the board in columns with names on them. At the top of the board is the phrase, "Honor Roll Students." I notice that there are three students' names on each piece of paper, and I wonder who they are. What does it mean to be on the Honor Roll? It seems like something strange, and I wonder what did they do to have their names on the board like that? I look around and there is no one to talk to, so I go to the chemistry class. Looking for a seat, I notice that there are three students sitting in the front row, and most of the other students sit back from *that* row of seats as if the seats themselves were bad signs. I go to the front and sit next to the other boy and ask him what the Honor Roll was and how did people get their names on it. He introduces himself as Rob, and I remember his name from the Honor Roll lists. The two girls sitting next to him, he says, are his cousins, and then he introduces me to them, I know that it was their names on those lists too, next to his; and they were the top three on all of the Honor Roll lists. The two girls look almost white, like Mrs. White. I begin asking Rob lots of questions, and the teacher is talking, but I can't shut up. He asks me to come to his home this weekend and says that we can have lots of fun doing homework together and he'll explain everything about the Honor Roll. We shake hands and promise to be friends forever. He says that we have to share each other's blood to make sure that we will always be friends. So, he gets a safety pin from one of his cousins and sticks his finger and sticks my finger. A little bubble of blood pops out of each of our fingers and we press our blood together. Now, he says, we are friends *forever*!

Getting home after school, I am excited and rush to tell Mother about Rob and his cousins, the Honor Roll, and how he invited me to come and spend the weekend at his house so we can talk about homework and lots of other things. She says, "*Good*, the White people won't know where you are out there, and they might not come and castrate you for looking at that naked *White* girl!" The next day is Friday, and I pack some clothes in a grocery bag for the weekend at Rob's house and the chance to see his cousins. I take the school bus with Rob and his cousins at the end of the day, and we go to their homes far away out in the country. When the bus stops and we get off, we walk slowly toward the driveway to their houses. The driveway opens into a large, large open space almost the size of the cottonfield. The grass is trimmed, pretty, and green. Rob points to one big house and says that this is his house and, looking at his cousins, says that they live in the house next door. The two houses look about the same size, and he says that they have their own private study rooms filled with books and study desks with lots of writing paper and pencils.

The girls walk on toward their house. I look at one of them and she looks back at me, smiling. I want to talk to her sooo much. She has pretty legs and long dark hair. Rob says, "Hey, let's go inside. I wanna show you something!" I follow him inside his house, looking back at the pretty girl walking away. We walk into his living room, and I am seeing a big brown sofa with cushion seats and large chairs. The living room is about the size of our front room and kitchen put together. He walks on into another room, and I am still looking at all the big things in the living room. "Come on," he says. I follow him into the next room, and he says that this one is his study room, and that his parents have their bedroom on the other side of the house. We look at his study desk with the sharp pencils and writing paper, his chair, and the big thing he calls an atlas map that is a round ball on a stand across the room. Looking at the atlas map, he spins it, and the ball goes around while he talks about the different countries

Man of the House

on it. Each country seems to have a different color, and I glance at his bookshelves and all of the books on them. I walk to the bookshelf and look at each book until I hear him calling from another room and go to see what he is showing me. I want to go back to the bookshelf, and he is talking about the Honor Roll now. He tells me about his study time and the big radio in his study room, how he studies when he gets home after school, and when he eats dinner with his parents, and lots of other things. Over the weekend, I do not see his cousins again until we head out of his door to get back on the bus on Monday morning. We spend the weekend talking about books, studying, and the Honor Roll.

His parents own their farm, and he says that he does not have to work until he finishes school. Everything is quiet here, and he says that he does not have any friends, so we have to be blood friends forever! His living room, the study room, and his bedroom all have big lights in the ceiling with strings to pull and make the lights come on at night, like Mama's house, and he has a big black telephone in his study room too. When I get back home, I rush to tell Mother about Rob and his cousins, and the Honor Roll, and everything! She looks at me and says, "Check on the kids and keep your eyes open because they might want to castrate you *for 'eye-raping' that White girl*." She says, "They *murdered* the Emmett Till kid when he 'eye-raped' a White girl." She scares me with these stories, and I get nightmares almost every night and I do not want to go to sleep. I go outside and sometimes in the woods in front of our house past the pasture.

One bright Sunday morning, Mother is sitting on the front porch patting a church fan against her knees. A stately light-complexioned Black man walks from the direction of Old Hank's house toward our house. Mother sees him and begins crossing her feet and stops fanning her knees. I am watching her slowly fan her face and smile at the man. He turns, smiling back at Mother, and walks into our yard and onto the porch and talks to Mother. A long black snake runs across the front yard behind him, and Mother yells to me, "Kill that snake!" I leave them, noticing that the man has green eyes, and go on to kill the snake. The man bows as he gets closer to Mother and smiles. She smiles too. They go inside of the house together, and I can soon smell the fragrance of coffee. The old bedsprings screech and I know what they are doing. I go to the woods for a while, and hours later, I go back in the house and see the two of them asleep on the bed, wrapped in each other's arms.

I go back outside and sit on the edge of the front porch. The other kids are in the backyard playing. When the man with the green eyes comes out, he sits next to me and tells me that his name is Emperor and that his son's name is Lil Emperor, because they have the same name. He says that he just got into the habit of calling him Lil Emperor so everyone would know him from his son. He says that his wife has died and that he owns lots of land not so far away and that I'll be able to find it easily because it is a brick house on a hill. He says that he has horses like the ones out there in that pasture, pointing to Ron's horses, and that he harvests his own crops. We shake hands and walk around on the side of the house where I had built an aviary and housed thirteen different-colored pigeons. He says that he likes birds and tells me that I did a good job building the aviary. I notice that he is wearing shiny tall boots and good clothes. Mother walks out of the house now, and he goes to her.

The White family living in the house on the hill just behind the old drunk's house is moving as Emperor is leaving Mother. My little friend with the short arm waves as their truck goes by our house, and I wave back to him. He waves with his short arm this time. The first time we met he kept this arm behind his back. About a month after this family moves away, Ron tells me that we can have the house they moved out of. It has two bedrooms, and when I tell Mother, she is happy. If Emperor ever comes back to visit Mother, he'll see an empty house.

Ron uses his pick-up truck to help us move to the house behind the drunk's house. There is a cow in the backyard, lots of hens, and a rooster. He teaches me how to milk the cow, and we have fresh milk to drink now. I find a small round barrel-shaped thing with a plunger sticking out of it that I learn to use to churn the milk and make buttermilk. All this new food, right in the backyard, and Mother smiles sometimes now. She wants to have a garden again, and I use the tractor to plow the garden for her. When we are not working in the cottonfields, Mother spends a lot of time in her garden growing okra, snap beans, butter beans, watermelons, cucumbers, turnip, collard, cabbage greens, onions, green pepper, and other vegetables from seeds I get from the general store. We do not have to eat grass, polk salad, and weeds with fat-back anymore. In the other house, we often ate grass when there was no food, and Mother would call it greens to keep my siblings from asking questions about what they were eating, after running in from school. Now we have chickens, eggs for breakfast, with grits or oatmeal, margarine, seasonings from the store, and when the cotton has been harvested, we all go back to school.

One Saturday, Ron asks me to take a load of hay, which is sitting in front of the big barn across from old drunk's house, and stack it in the barn. Will wants to help me, and we go to the barn together and throw the hay off the trailer into the first floor of the barn. Then we start taking the bales, one by one, up to the second floor. The ground floor is used to stack any other things Ron wants to put there. Old Hank wobbles over with a Mason jar of whiskey in his right hand and begins yelling, "Hey, niggurs! Al'll come up thar'n *cut yer nuts out*! Whut cha'll durin' up thar anyways?" I walk to the edge of the second floor and look down at Drunk with the pitchfork in my right hand. "Whut chu thank yer gon do wid that thar pitchfork, *boy*?!!" he demands. "I'll come up thar 'n rip yer ferkin hearts ait!" I look at him, knowing that he can barely walk and that he is not going to hurt anyone.

We stare at each other, and I tell him, "You're not going to do anything because I'll take this pitchfork and *gouge your eyes out*!" I know that he cannot go and tell any other White person what I have said because no one will believe him.

"*Do you know I'm ur Whiiite man, boy?! You don't talk ter me lak that, niggur!*" I stare at him, holding the pitchfork, and he begin wobbling backwards a bit and then turns and wobbles on back home.

We live in the house on the hill behind the drunk for a short time. Christmas comes, and Ron hands me a big, white sack and tells me, "These are some Christmas toys for y'all." I thank him and take the sack home to Mother and tell her what he said. Her face brightens until she empties the sack and sees that there are lots of old worn-out dolls in it. I go to the seed store and get a batch of seeds to sell. In making my rounds to the houses I usually go to, I stop to ask Mrs. Kasey if she wants to buy any for the coming season. Tee comes in the room, and we leave to let Mrs. Kasey look over the seeds. We sit on the sofa and talk for a little while and go back to her aunt. Always short on money, I walk the gravel roads during the evenings and weekends looking for empty soft drink bottles and cans to take to the general store to trade. The store pays me a penny for each glass soft drink bottle and one penny for two empty cans. I buy oatmeal, margarine, rice, flour, meal, and other food items.

Man of the House

During Presidents' month, I sketch cars and images of US presidents and offer to sell them to teachers to put on their classroom windows. One teacher buys one of the presidents for ten cents. The other teachers only smile and say no.

I sell these small packages of garden seeds for five cents and look for other work. Now the fall is here, we do not have anything from Mother's garden, and most times we eat oatmeal, grits, eggs, and what I can buy from the store after I sell bottles, cans, and seeds. Mother says that the stork will soon bring us another sister or brother too. Sometimes I buy meat, cornmeal, self-rising flour, dried beans, and peas from the grocery store. Food is easy to get this way, and the winter is passing.

Mother has six boys and three girls now. She says that before I was born, she had three stillborn babies. Prince is eight years old now, and he is always weak. His eyes are weak, and he is skinny. When I am home, he stays close to me, holding onto my pocket with his right hand while sucking his thumb on the other hand. We are best friends too. One day, I search for empty bottles and cans and make enough money to buy him a small red battery radio. He looks at it and his little eyes become bright. I turn it on, and he hears voices coming out of it. He presses it close to his right ear and tells me, "They are *talking to me*! They are *singing to me*!" He does not suck his thumb anymore. Whenever I am home, he runs to tell me, "They are talking to me! They are singing to me!" I tell him that it is a radio, and he says, "I know. People in there talking to me. They sing to me. I know." Late one afternoon, Prince becomes ill, and Mother says that he has a high fever and that we have to get him to the doctor's office. The nearest doctor is six miles away in Charleston and we have no transportation. The general store is about two miles away, and I pick Prince up and we begin walking the long gravel road to the general store to get help.

Prince seems to weigh more and more as we walk. Sometimes we have to stop, rest, and then walk on again until I get him to the store. Prince's little body keeps growing heavier and heavier as I walk and stumble on gravel rocks in the winding gravel road. The sun is going down behind the trees, and night begins to fall as we enter the store. My arms and shoulders feel numb as I lay Prince on the table in the back of the store and watch the storekeeper rush for a tub and ice to put him in. His little body is soon covered in ice, and he pleads

Man of the House

for his radio. I pull the radio from my pocket, turn it on, and put it next to his right ear and watch his small face turn into a weak smile. Mother is praying, and Prince's eyes close in death. She cries and everyone knows that he is dead. We do not know about the White doctor in town. Mother cries, and the storekeeper wrings her little white hands until they turn red. Mother's whole body shakes as she kisses Prince good-bye and begins walking outside. We take him out of the ice, and the storekeeper cries, "He's cold! *Let me get a blanket!*" She comes rushing back with the blanket, and we cover Prince with his radio, then go outside and I borrow their shovel and dig his little grave. The storekeeper comes to the door and says, "Come get your brother and bring him outside with us while you get his grave ready. *Put him right over there!*"

I dig his grave, and just as I am about to put him in it with his radio, the storekeeper says, "Wait! Let me go get some croaker sacks so you don't have to put him on the bare ground." She rushes back out with croaker sacks and gives them to me to line Prince's grave. I lay him in the grave, wrapped in the wet blanket he was wrapped in inside the tub of ice. After covering his grave, the storekeeper prays for him, and we embrace. "I'm sorry," she says, "I'm so *sorry!*" We look at each other. I walk away to take Mother home. I return to school.

It is about three a.m. one morning when Mother's ear-gripping scream wakes me, and I bolt out of bed and run to see what is happening. "*The baby is coming!*" she says. "Put some water on the stove and go get the midwife!" Confused, I rush outback and pump water in a bucket, bring it back inside, and put it on the stove. "*Hurry!*" she cries. "Get the midwife, *Lord Jesus*! Did you put the water on the stove?!" I light the wood in the stove and run to get dressed. "Get the midwife!?" she screams, and I rush out the front door, running for Mrs. Kasey's house. I do not know what a "midwife" is, and Mother is screaming.

Tee opens the door and I ask her what a midwife is. Her eyes get big, and she calls, "Mama!" looking back over her shoulder. Mrs. Kasey comes to the door, and I tell her that Mother is screaming and told me to go get the midwife. She tells me where the midwife lady lives and says, "Hurry, son!"

When we get back to the house, the baby's head is out and Mother is still screaming, taking deep breaths and groaning! The veins on her forehead and neck seem about to burst. Her knees are up and legs open. There is blood on

Man of the House

the bed, and the midwife hisses, "Get some water on the stove! We gonna need some hot water!" I run into the kitchen and bring out the hot water. She holds the baby's head and slowly moves her. The baby slips out of Mother, and the midwife says to me, "Come har 'n hold de baby's head so's hit don't fall! I gots-tu help yo' mama git ur de affer-birf!" The baby is out all the way, and the midwife works feverishly to clean Mother, clean the baby, and cut the long, white cord. I stand there holding a new baby and inhaling the fresh fragrance of blood. The midwife takes out the afterbirth package and keeps cleaning Mother. "Now, go bury dis!" she says, taking the baby from me and giving me the afterbirth package wrapped in a big rag.

When I get back inside, Mother says to me, "Go tell your sisters and brothers that *the stork* just brought you all another little sister!" I stare at her, knowing now how all the babies got in our house, and knowing that I just heard her say to me, "Go tell your sisters and brothers that the stork just brought you all another little sister!" Still, I go in the bedroom and tell them what she said. Daylight is dawning and I walk outside, and I feel nervous and scared. I notice blood on my hands and light a cigarette. I feel numb in the dawning morning, glued to the porch and watching the cigarette smoke curling as it goes into the morning air. I am seventeen years old, and now I know there is no stork. No stork, I hear myself saying. No stork. I remember Mother and me walking the gravel road in Shelby, and a lady is walking slowly toward us, and Mother tells me, "Look at that lady there with the big stomach. She swallowed a watermelon seed!" Mother laughed when she said that. I dreamed a lot of dreams back then with ladies swallowing watermelon seeds and big green vines growing out of them and the watermelons on the vines.

"Ouch!" the cigarette burns my fingers. I have forgotten that I have it in my hand and it is burned up. I smoke Winston cigarettes now 'cause the other boys at school say that only faggots do not smoke. Real men smoke cigarettes. I do not want to be a "faggot," and I started smoking last year, and Mother said it was okay. I light another cigarette and smoke it now, thinking about how I lied to my brothers and sisters about the stork. I am remembering lots of stories Mother has told me now, and I do not know if they are true or not. Maybe the story about Emmett Till is not true? I am not sure. I remember when Mother told me that Santa Clause came down the chimney while we were sleeping, got a slice of the chocolate cake, and then left because he forgot to bring us toys. That Christmas, I had cooked the cake and saw her walking on tiptoes going in the kitchen, cutting a slice for herself, eating it, and going back to bed. I light another cigarette. I saw my sister come right out of Mother; so why did she lie to me? I wonder. She calls me and says that I have to go to the general store and call Mama and tell her about the new baby and ask her to come and stay with us awhile. Mama comes, and the midwife leaves. A man is driving a truck and Mama is sitting beside him.

Chapter 7
Back to School

*Love does no thinking.
It waits with soul, with me,
weeping in this corner.*
— Rumi

We move back to Shelby. Now we live on "The Sixteen Section" gravel road in a white house with a tree on the side. We have two bedrooms now. Mother sleeps in the living room and we sleep in the two bedrooms. The kitchen is behind the first bedroom, and we have only two beds: one for Mother and one for our bedroom. At night, all the kids scramble to get in the bed 'cause nobody wants to sleep on the floor with just blankets. Mother gets a big brown radio for her room, and now she listens to a radio story every night called "The Shadow Knows," and it is scary. She tells everyone to come in the living room when her story starts, and she will not let us talk while the story is on the radio. We rush to bed then, and lots and lots of tiny brown bugs come out and bite us and drink our blood. Mother calls them bed bugs. They make us wake up and slap ourselves trying to get them off. Every night, we get eaten by the bed bugs. Daylight comes and I look around everywhere and see two houses not far from us. One day, a school bus comes by our house, and Mother tells us that we can go to school at Broad Street School when there is no work to do.

Man of the House

I enter Broad Street High School as a junior. Mother reminds me that I am still responsible for making sure all the kids get on and off the bus when leaving and coming back home. The first day of school, I go to my homeroom to get books I will use for the year, and my homeroom teacher, Mrs. Vanila, tells us that the books are piled on the floor at the back of the room. She says that they were brought here from the White school, that the White school gets new books every year, and that the books their kids used the previous year are brought to our school for us to use, and we will have to pick out the best ones that do not have pages torn out or damaged. I rush to the pile and pick out my books, afraid that other students will beat me to the best ones. I pile the books in my arms and get off the floor, take my seat in the class, and notice that the other students are still chatting and laughing just inside the classroom. The bell rings for us to go to our second class, and as I walk out through the door, someone grabs my genitals. I look to the right and see Diff running away, grinning. It was Diff who ran to tell my Mama that I was having sex with the babysitter when I was five years old. I tell Mrs. Vanila. She looks away and tells me to go to my next class.

I get to Professor Davis's classroom and sit on one of the front row seats. He talks about the New Farmers of America (NFA) program and asks for candidates to go with him to the next statewide meeting. I raise my hand, and he says that he wants me to be the school's local chapter secretary too. I jump for the offer. As the class is ending, he asks me to stay behind. Other students file out of the class, laughing and talking. Prof. Davis goes behind his desk and returns with a box. He opens it, and there is a small, red pig inside of the box. He asks me to take it home and raise it and says that if I do a good job raising and grooming the pig, he'll take me to the agricultural fair in Memphis next year. "It is a Duroc Show Pig," he says. "I got it from Dr. Hood in Mound Bayou." When I get home, I tell Mother about the pig and show it to her. She just looks at me. Then I tell her that Diff grabbed me down there. She smirks her face and says "God does not like that! Clean the kitchen and cook dinner when you get through with that pig." On many days to come when leaving this homeroom class, Diff does the same thing. When I tell the principal, he just says, "Go to class. I am busy!"

I tell Mama and she says, "He is nasty."

Man of the House

One day, I go to the boys' toilet and see Diff giving some other boys whiskey to drink while he plays with their genitals. I leave the boys' toilet and go to my class. During the year, I study the galaxies in my science class. I carve the names of the stars of the Milky Way on the front side of the box, make the short pieces to separate the front from the back side of the box, and take the pieces to my science teacher. In science class, I study the major stars and planets and paint my box pieces blue. During the year in this class, I screw electrical wires from each star in the galaxy and screw the other end of the wire to the answer for the correct star on the other side of the front of the box, with a central wire going from a battery to a buzzer. When it is finished, I test the connections and the buzzer goes off when I touch the right answer for each star. My teacher is happy at the end of the year and takes me to the science fair in Memphis.

In my agriculture class this year, I study how to take care of my pig once I've gotten her in a pen behind the house. Building the pen is fun. She watches me make it for her. She stands there with the little rope around her back and underneath her front legs, and tied to one of the posts. Sometimes she gives me a piggy grunt, then eats and falls asleep. Once she is in her pen, I go to the dry cleaners and get a job to buy her food. I work here on Saturdays, pressing white garments for the hospital in Mound Bayou. In school, Prof. Davis teaches me the parliamentary rules from Robert's Rules of Order, helps me to buy a New Farmers of America jacket to promote the organization at school, and he teaches me what the organization does, how it operates, and teaches me how to take care of my growing show pig. Time passes, and she grows fast and pretty. In English class, Mrs. Brown teaches us cursive writing. She calls me to the front of the class one morning, and just as I am passing one girl with a low-cut blouse, I see her breasts and ask if I can touch them. She says, *"NO!"* and I do it anyway. She cuts my right arm with a razor blade, and I go on to see what Mrs. Brown wants. She teaches me how to write in cursive on the blackboard. I wipe the blood from my arm while writing, and on my way back to my seat, I ask the girl who cut me what is her name. She turns away and I go on to my seat. It feels like lunch time because my stomach is growling. Mrs. Brown picks up a Coke bottle from the side of her desk, takes the top off, and pours a small package of Planter's Peanuts into it, then raises the bottle to her mouth and drinks it down. I hear the Coke bubbling out of the bottle as it takes the peanuts down Mrs. Brown's throat. The bell rings and we stream out of her class for lunch. Everyday Mrs. Brown ends her class this way, and the bell rings almost as soon as she finishes drinking down the peanut-filled Coke.

Back home, I am feeding my show pig and see an opossum crossing the yard and hear Mother yell, "Kill it and bring it in the house! We've got to have some meat for dinner!" I kill the opossum, and after cleaning it, I bring it to her. She is excited to have meat for dinner and starts cooking it, joking that it looks like a little baby in the pot with its head sticking above the water. She dances about the kitchen, cooking and happy about the meat for dinner. I go back outside and walk my pig around the pen like Prof. Davis taught me to do. Then I feed her and go inside to study. The time for cotton picking is almost over, and most of my siblings go to the fields with Mother. I do not go to the fields anymore, because each time I lift the cotton sack up to the top of the trailer to dump it, my hernia bulges out in extreme pain and I must lie down under the tall cotton stalks on my sack to rest until it stops hurting.

The following year, my science teacher takes me and a few other students to the science fair in Memphis, and I win a first prize ribbon for my project. Once back home, I place my project near the open door near Mother's room and ask her to watch it for me while I do my chores. When I return inside of the house, I find only splinters of my project scattered near the place where I left it and ask Mother what happened to it. Without looking at me, she says, "Dred broke it up." He is one of my younger half-brothers and she allowed him to destroy my science first prize. I walk back outside and groom my now large Duroc Show sow. Prof. Davis takes me to the NFA's state-wide annual conference at Alcorn College. We walk from his car, across campus, and I see students sitting alone or as couples on the manicured lawns. Some sit with their backs against trees, reading books. One stately man with books under his right arm walks toward us and says, "Morning, Prof. Davis," and now I know how he got that name. He smiles and nods to the other man and we keep walking until we get to one brick building and go inside, take our seats, and listen to someone at the podium talk about the organization. He talks slowly and calmly about the organization's plans to merge with the Future Farmers of America, then asks for candidates for the coming year's officers.

Man of the House

He tells us that he is a candidate for president, and Prof. Davis touches my shoulder and says, "Aren't you a candidate for vice president?" I raise my hand and tell the president that I am a candidate for vice president. It is a spontaneous decision. I feel the eyes of others staring at me and two others raise their hands to challenge me. We must come up to the podium and talk about what makes us the better one for the position. I am elected vice president of the organization. Prof. Davis talks about each of the big brick buildings as we walk back to his car. I see other Blacks walking gracefully across this manicured lawn to go in or come out of these large buildings on this college campus, like it is just normal. There is a rainbow of colors in people here. They do not seem to fear being castrated here either. The whole campus feels safe.

I am happy. I look around and see Prof. Davis smiling. I am happy to be on a college campus, and it feels great to be vice president too. I never heard of a "college" before, and I am *here*! When he talked to me about "going to Alcorn," he had not said the word "college," and now I know and ask him about how people get into a college. He says that I will have to apply to get in and have money to pay to be here studying. When we get back to school, he tells me to get my Duroc Show Pig ready to go to Memphis for the annual livestock fair. I walk her around and around her pen each day until Prof. Davis comes to the house and takes us to the great livestock fair in Memphis. We walk together slowly around the ring at the fair, and she wins first prize. Once Prof. Davis takes me and my first-prize Duroc friend back home, I take her out of the trailer, thank him, and walk her past the tree on the side of the house, on toward the backyard toward her pen. Mother yells at me, "*Kill that hog*! We need meat on the table!" I stop and look at her. "*You heard me*," she yells, "Kill that hog! *Kill that hog! We need meat on the table! I'm your mother! Now do what I say!*" I get on my knees and talk to her about what Mother is demanding me to do. Her smiling eyes do not tell me that she understands.

I tied her to one of the posts of her pen and go inside of the house to get a butcher's knife, then back outside and get on my knees in front of her and shove the knife into her throat until it slashes her heart. She grunts once, and her eyes begin closing as her blood flows out of the wound. She lays down on the ground, and I begin building a scaffold to raise her off the ground so that I can pour scalding hot water over her to get the hair off her skin. Once all

Man of the House

her hair is off, I cut her open down the center of her belly, take out her heart, intestines, liver, and everything and take them inside to Mother. She is excited and begins talking to herself about all the meat she will have for the year. I cut the pig's body into separate parts and take each piece into the kitchen and put it on the kitchen table, and once it is full, I put the other pieces on the floor. Mother starts cooking her right away and making dinner for everyone. I go back outside and clean away everything that she had and burn it. When I get back inside the kitchen, Mother says, "Sit down and eat your dinner!" I look around and tell her that I cannot eat that. "Are you disobeying me?!" she demands, and stares at me. I look into her eyes and do not say anything.

She gets her extension cord, doubles it, and starts beating me. I stand still and do not feel anything. *"You're not going to cry, huh?"* she says, smirking her face. I can only look at her. Tears go down my throat and hurt. I cannot talk. She does not hit me anymore, and I walk into the bedroom and lie on the bed.

Uncle Brutte comes to visit Mama and Mother. One day, he comes to our house and tells me that we need to have a man-to-man talk. He and Mother talk for a little while, and then he and I walk along the dirt road from our house toward Broad Street School. The sky is clear, and the sun is shining softly on the earth. "I'd fuck a snake right now if I could get somebody to hold its head!" he says, and laughs. A snake. . . I wonder how he can do that? "When you finish school," he starts, "you gotta come to Chicago and live with me and my girl. They got naked White women up there hanging out of apartment windows and you can fuck 'em all you wonts to!" He laughs again. I see images of naked White women with their legs hanging out of windows in big buildings. I do not know what to say. I have never seen naked women hanging out of windows.

We turn left on another dirt road, and it is quiet. He is wearing his khaki shirt and pants, his shoes are black and shining in the sunlight, and he says, "You see that sign upper head uv us?"

I say, "Yes, sir."

He looks at me, frowning, and says, "You don't say no fucking 'Yes, sir' to me, man. We jes talking. You say 'Yeah or Naw,' know what I'm sayin'?"

I say, "Yes, sir,…I mean, 'Yes.'"

Man of the House

He smiles and says, "Na, you see that fuckin' sign there," pointing to a stop sign, and tells me, "Those letters mean 'State Taxes On Pussy!' And you bess remember that!" We turn on the road where Beauty and Mama live, and he says, "Na, I gots to go n' git me some *pussy*! Remember, when you finish school, I want you to come to Chicago 'n' live with me, and you can fuck ur-bunch of White girls up there! Now, you go one way, 'n' I'm going another 'cause I gotta git me some *pussy*! I'll see you in Chicago!" We shake hands, smiling, and he tiptoes off along the dirt road in front of Mama's house, going toward my godmother's house. He walks on his tiptoes, like he is worried about his shoes getting dirt on them.

I am still working in the Miller's Dry Cleaning place. I work here every weekday now till school starts and I get into my senior year of classes. It is hotter in the dry cleaner than it is in the cottonfield. Hot air blows around and around in the little building, and I am working near the front pressing white clothes for the hospital in Mound Bayou. My first cousin, SpyMain, lives in Mama's house now and rides around a lot with other boys. Sometimes they get together and sing gospel songs or drink whiskey and laugh and talk together in the road. He does not go to school anymore. Mama told Mother that he dropped out of school in the eighth grade, like Uncle Brutte did, and that he is going into the army soon. He and his friends drive a black-and-white Ford car too, and go to lots of places, like Winstonville, Mound Bayou, and even Greenville where my Dad used to live. One day, I see him with Diff at school, and he says, "What chu gon do fur lunch?" and I tell him that I'm going to Mama's house and see if she has any food in the refrigerator. "I'll beat chu there," he says, grinning, and we break out through the front door of the school, running like crazy to get to Mama's house. Most times, she has one box of chocolate milk and one box of white milk, and we both want the chocolate milk.

I beat him into the backdoor of the house, push open the door to the kitchen, and get the chocolate milk box. "We got to wrestle fur dat milk," he says, grinning. "How 'bout you put dat milk on the table, and the one that wins the wrestle gits the milk?"

I say, "Okay," and we wrestle.

I get him down on the floor and he yells, "Main, you choking me!" I release him, and he shoves me over and jumps up, grabs the milk, grinning, and yells, "I got dis shit ni!" and runs out of the house. Almost every day at school he meets me at my classroom door, and we do the same thing. One night, he asks me to come with him and Dudds to practice singing. I go with them, and I do not know the songs they are practicing and leave, walk back home, and get my book and flashlight. Mother comes into the bedroom on her way to the kitchen and says, "They're scrapping cotton tomorrow and we can make a little money!" I do not say anything. The next morning, I go to school and Mother takes the others to the cottonfield to scrap cotton.

Back in school, Prof. Davis tells me to make sure I wear the black windbreaker with the New Farmers of America in gold letters across the back and NFA in gold letters on the front. Then he tells me that the New Farmers of America and the Future Farmers of America will be making plans to merge someday, so we must talk about what we're going to do. In my mathematics class, the teacher is Mr. Crip. He is new, and his brother, John, is new too. I have not been to school for a while, and when I go to Mr. Crip's class, I have not gotten a book to read for today's lesson and he looks around the class, points at me, and says, "Go to the blackboard! You! I'm going to give you a problem to solve!" Nervous, I go to the blackboard and write out the problem he reads to me. I cannot think. I am nervous and stand looking at the problem and wondering what to do to solve it. My knees are shaking as I hear him yell, "Sit down, *fool*!" Mortified and humiliated, I go back to my seat and sit down. I am glad when the school day ends, and we get on the bus and go home. Mother does not say anything when I get home. She cooks dinner and tells everyone to come and eat. I see a big slice of my Duroc show pig on the table and turn to go back to the bedroom. She yells, "*I said come in here and eat your food*! Now, *get back in here and eat! I am your mother and your daddy, too!*" I eat the vegetables and leave the room. She is angry, and I feel sick in my stomach.

Next morning, she tells me to make sure all the children get on and off the bus today. The school bus stops in front of our house, and I wait till everyone else is on it and then I step up into the bus. A big man is driving the bus. Zarv is talking to somebody, and they laugh really loud. The bus driver stops and asks who was that making all that noise? He is looking at me, and I do not say anything. When he parks the bus in front of the school, he tells me to hold back and let the others get off the bus. I am nervous. All the other kids get off the bus, and he grabs my shirt collar and pulls me to a white building on the side of the school, in through the door, and shoves me ahead. I stumble and then get straightened up, look at the teacher behind the desk and all of the kids in the room. The big bus driver says, "Git cho ass down on the flo'!" I look at the teacher with the mean face, and then on her desk I see a strap made out of a piece of a cotton gin belt with a stick on it and the belt end is split like a snake's tongue. The big bus driver walks closer, as if he is going to kick me or something worse. The teacher walks around her desk and says, "Turn over on your stomach!"

She beats me with the thick strap, and the big bus driver stands a little distance away with his feet apart and his hands almost in a fist. She keeps beating and I pee on myself and start to feel numb. She goes on beating and telling me to keep my mouth shut when I am on the bus! I do not know how long she beats me before she stops and tells me to get off her floor and go to class. My pants are really wet, and my shirt is sticking to my skin. I can just barely walk, and when I get back to my class, the teacher and kids stare at me. I hear one kid saying to someone, "*He's been to Mrs. Cat's room for a beatin' and I know hur! She-ur kill you, boy!*" I find an empty seat near the back of the classroom and sit down and have to get back up because I am too sore to sit down. The teacher looks at me and says, "*Take your seat!*" and I sit back in the seat. Soon I do not feel the seat, and when the class is over, I sneak out the door next to the cafeteria and go home. I have to keep my legs wide apart when I walk because my pants are wet and blood-stained. My shirt is sticking to my skin, and I hurt everywhere. When I tell Mother about the teacher who beat me, she says that the bus drive is her husband, and his name is Duffus. Then she says, "You *must have done something wrong*!"

I go to my first class next morning and watch the teacher as she moves on her desk like she is getting comfortable, and in this quiet morning air, I look to see what she is doing, moving about on the desk. Most times when she moves, it is not like she kinda half-rolls her body to one side, like maybe one of her legs has gone to sleep and she is trying to wake it up or something. I am sitting in the far back right corner of her class and I can see everything she is doing because there is nobody sitting in front of me. Mrs. Fine is tall, and every day she wears a dress that falls just below her knees. When she crosses her legs, the dress moves up to just above her knees. When it is quiet like this and there is nothing to do, my eyes follow her movement, like they've got to know what she is doing.

"Come here, you *nasty boy* in the back!" she yells at me. Everybody turns to look at me when she yells. I walk up to her desk. "Come with me," she says, sternly. "I am taking you to the superintendent's office. *You are nasty!* You are supposed to be studying your history!" I hear some of the girls giggling, and I feel ashamed and confused. I do not like to be called nasty, and I do not know what wrong thing I did. Mother and Mama say that boys are nasty, too. "Walk faster," Mrs. Fine says, "I have to get back to my class." We get to the office, and she stops and waves me ahead of her, pushes my shoulder to make me go ahead. In the office, she says to the superintendent, her husband, "This boy is nasty." He turns up his nose as she shoves me to his desk. She leaves the office. Mr. Fine is writing on a short piece of white paper. Then he folds the white paper and says to me, "Take this note home to your mother and tell her you have been suspended from school for three days for acting nasty in Mrs. Fine's class. Get out of here!" I leave school and walk out of the front doors. Everything seems quiet out here. The morning sun is hiding behind the clouds and there is no wind. It is getting hot, and there is no one out in the road playing. The grown folks might have gone to the cottonfields. It is quiet, and I go home.

When I go back to school, it is almost time to graduate. My homeroom teacher, Mrs. Vanila, gives me a part in the graduation play and tells the class who is our valedictorian, salutatorian, and, pointing at me, says, "He is our Student Most Likely to Succeed for the year." Will has been helping to get our siblings on the school bus and back home for a little while now. I walk over to Mama's house to talk to SpyMain and his friends. Today the roads are quiet, and I do not see any adults sitting on their front porches. The air feels uneasy, and I am not sure what has happened. I get near Mama's house and see one of the Jasper kids who live next door to her and ask where is everybody. She says, "It was an *accident! He is blind and he didn't see the boy!*"

I ask, "What accident?"

And she says, "E. H. *accidentally* shot that boy! *It was an accident!*" and she turns away and goes back inside her house. SpyMain is not home, and I tell Mama that Jessica said that Mr. E. H. shot and killed a kid. She frowns and looks through me with cold eyes. She says, "*You better not ever let me hear you say anything about Mr. E. H. again*! He's *blind* and that boy must have got in the way or Lord *knows what! It's in the White folks' hands now. Get home to your mother!*" Walking home slowly, I remember that it was not long ago when I heard that "somebody stabbed D.C. in the back with an ice pick and he died, too." I don't know who the boy is that Mr. E. H. killed, and Mama had told me not to talk about D.C. when he was killed, too. She had said, "We are not supposed to talk about what goes on in *our neighborhood*."

Mother is home when I get back, and she looks away when I walk in the house. I had my pistol that I bought to make Diff keep his hands off me. Z.Z. stopped the car on the side of the road, and as soon as Diff started grinning and grabbing after my pants, I pulled my gun on him and told him that if he touched me, I would kill him. As soon as we got back to Mama's house that night, SpyMain ran in and told Mama that I had a gun. She demanded to see it and took it away from me, threw it down into the outhouse; and SpyMain grinned, leaving the house to go back out with his friends. One occasion, while sitting and reading in Lawyer Dunbar's office, I had felt the presence of someone near, and looking out of the side window, I'd see SpyMain's head peeking through the window. Later, Mother would tell me that he had told her what he saw me doing in that lawyer's office.

Chapter 8
Sometimes It Be's That Way

*We're strangers here where we never hear *yes*.*
We must be from some other town.
— Rumi

On May 19, 1963, I graduate from Broad Street High School, and I tell Mother to help me find my dad. She tells me the name of a gas station in Greenville where he works as a mechanic, and I take Will with me on the Greyhound bus to see him. It is quiet around the gas station when we get there. We walk in through the front door and on into the shop. He is working on the part of a car and looks up to see us. I tell him who we are and that I graduated from high school. He puts down his tools, walks around his work bench, takes out his wallet, and pulls a dollar bill out of it and hands it to me. Then he says, "I've got to get back to work." He turns away from us and goes back to his work. We are standing there looking at him work, and he does not see us. I turn and leave, and Will follows me out of the gas station, swearing that he is going to be a mechanic just like Daddy.

The next morning, I go out looking for a job. Walking along the sidewalk facing Highway 61, in front of the large bungalow houses owned by White, middle-class families, and I scan their houses and walk on toward town. By chance, I notice a sign in front of one big house that reads, "Painter Needed."

Man of the House

My Uncle Brutte had often told me he knows how to mix paint and paint houses. Remembering how I painted my science project, I go to the backdoor; a lady comes to the door and I ask if she still wants someone to paint her house. She says, "Yes!" and walks out slowly and goes to the back where she has a ladder, paint, brushes, and a stick to stir the paint. She is elderly and tells me how to stir the paint before taking it up on the ladder to paint the house from the top down.

I begin painting from the top down. By mid-morning, I get the hang of painting and like it. On my way back home after work that first day, I get to the road that Mama lives on and see a pretty lady standing beside a nice shiny car. I am looking at her and wondering who she is when a man sees me and yells, "You better git cho eyes off 'dat woman, boy! *She dat White main's woman! You git cho nuts cut off fur looking at dat gull!*" I ask what her name is, and he says "says 'Dat's dat Joyce, and she be datin' Baby Mike!" And day after day for the next two weeks, I paint the house from sunup till sundown. Early one morning, the lady walks out of her back door and congratulates me on the wonderful work I have been doing. She pays me $62.18, tells me to take a day off to rest and come back. I thank her for the job and the money, put the paint and ladder back in place, and make a B-line for the Greyhound bus stop. I buy my ticket to Chicago and run home to get my clothes and get back to the bus stop. The clerk said that the bus would be here around two o'clock. The bus ticket cost me eighteen dollars, and walking out of Mother's door, I hear her asking, "Where're you going?!"

I say, "Chicago."

She smiles and says, "Send me your address when you get settled!" I throw her a good-bye kiss and run back to the bus stop. The Greyhound bus arrives, and I get on and give the driver my ticket, walk toward the middle of the bus, and take a window seat. My heart throbs as the big bus moves off onto the highway and heads north. It is soon moving so fast until the trees and houses are zipping past us in the opposite direction. This is 1963.

I go straight to Uncle Brute's apartment when I get to Chicago, and his lady says that he is not home. "You might find him in one of the back alleys drunk or something. Put your things in the other room and rest a while. He'll be back sometime." They are living in an apartment near the corner of Homer

Man of the House

and Warren Blvd. After a nap, I go outside and walk around to look at the neighborhood and see Uncle Brute leaning against the wall of an apartment building, drunk, with a brown whiskey bottle in his left hand. It has rained and there is water on the concrete alley where he is sitting. "Hey, Main," he says, looking up at me. "Gimme two dollars! I gotta git me ur bottle." I ask if he wants to go home, and he says, "Yes, after I git me ur bottle." I give him two dollars and help him to get home.

When I wake the next morning, his lady says, "You better take your money and git ur place for yo-self 'cause yo Uncle will steal it and you'll never see that money again! Now, while he's sleeping, if I wuz you, I'd git outter here and find my own place!"

I pick up my bag and find a hotel that rents rooms by the week and go out job searching. I ask lots of people along the street how I might get a job quick because I do not have much money. One man tells me about a place that helps people find jobs and tells me how to get to that place. It is not far away, and I walk to it. The clerk tells me about a job opening, working on an assembly line making transformers, and I ask to have that job. She writes out a statement for me to take with me the next day and says she will call the company and tell them I am coming in to work and don't give the job to anybody else before they see me. Now I only must learn how to use the public buses to get to work and back to my hotel. The next day, I begin working for Transformers, Inc. on the northside of the city. First, I have to learn how to "punch a clock" before I can start working. And the supervisor tells me that they take "taxes" out of my paycheck before I get paid. Punching a clock is very strange, and somebody taking taxes seems foreign to me. At lunch time, I ask some of the other workers why do we have to put that card in the clock thing and punch in, and what is taking taxes before I get my money? They laugh and ask me where I am from. When I say Mississippi, they all laugh and tell me what the clock punching and taxes are and why I must give "the government money" before I get paid.

Uncle Brute finds me in the hotel and asks me to loan him twenty-five. I give him the money, and he wants me to go with him to have breakfast with his lady. She is waiting in the restaurant when we get there. She is not the same lady he lives with, and he introduces us. After breakfast, I search the neighborhood until I find an efficiency apartment and move into it. Now he does not know where I live and work. Looking around the neighborhood one day, I meet another guy who just got to Chicago from South Carolina, and he teaches me how to shoot pool. We go to the poolroom almost every evening after work and explore the neighborhood, meet girls, and talk about making lots of money. One day, I see Brute and we go to a restaurant to have a Cherry Coke and talk. He is sober and tells me that he just got out of the VA Hospital Rehab Center. He complains that they tied him down with leather straps in that place and made him get sober and says he'll never get drunk again. He wants to introduce me to his "girlfriend," he says, and we go to the southside of the city and meet her. She is nice. Her name is Fancy, and she gives us a soft drink and sits down, talking to Brute; and looking at me, she says, "He can't last as long as I can in bed!"

Brute says, "*That's a lie!*" They go to the bedroom, and now that it is getting late in the evening, I get on a bus to go back home. A pretty lady is looking at me, and I am looking at her, while I am putting the fare in the machine next to the driver. I sit beside her and notice that she has barbeque sauce on her white work-dress. We talk about her job cooking barbeque ribs, dating, and money till she gets near her apartment on the Westside and invites me to walk her home. Her name is Mary Baker, and we make plans to meet the next day and go to her brother's party at his apartment. We date for the coming year and have lots of fun until she tells me that she cheated on me and that she is sorry. We make up and continue dating.

It is late on an afternoon when I hear a steady knock on my front door, open it, and see Mother standing there, smiling, saying, "*I made it!*" Walking in my apartment, past me with her bags, she says, "I told Will to sell everything and take the money and bring the other children up here." She goes on into my bedroom and falls asleep. I sleep on the sofa, and the next morning when I wake up, she is gone. It is early April 1964 when I get back from work and Mother tells me that she has gotten a job cleaning somebody's house and "we need to get a bigger apartment before Will gets here with the others." We find a three-bedroom apartment and move in. About a month later, Will and all the others get to Chicago, and now the whole family is here.